How To Make Your Own Picture Frames

**Step-by-step pictures of
Over 50 basic frame styles
And how to finish them**

For Artists—Students—Photographers—Decorators—Home
Craftsmen

**Hal Rogers
Ed Reinhardt**

 Watson-Guptill Publications
New York

To Irene and Margaret, who as wives were understanding . . . as "authors' widows" were patient . . . as critics, unmerciful!

Copyright © 1958 by Harold L. Rogers and Edwin P. Reinhardt

First published 1958 in New York by Watson-Guptill Publications,
a division of Billboard Publications, Inc.,
1515 Broadway, New York, N.Y. 10036

Library of Congress Catalog Card Number: 64-23733
ISBN 0-8230-2450-4

Manufactured in U.S.A.

First Edition, 1958
Revised, Enlarged Edition, 1964
First Printing, 1964
Second Printing, 1966
Third Printing, 1967
Fourth Printing, 1970
Fifth Printing, 1972
Sixth Printing, 1974
Seventh Printing, 1975
Eighth Printing, 1976
Ninth Printing, 1976
Tenth Printing, 1977
Eleventh Printing, 1979
Twelfth Printing, 1981

Introduction

Hal Rogers and Ed Reinhardt are eminently qualified experts on picture-framing — both from the craftsman's standpoint — they have been making their own handsome frames for years — and from the esthetic standpoint — both are accomplished professional artists.

Hal Rogers joined the Royal Canadian Air Force shortly before Pearl Harbor, and was eventually placed in charge of an R.C.A.F. Art Department in Ottawa. After the war, he studied at Pratt Institute, free-lanced, and worked as Assistant Art Director for an advertising agency. After several years as Art Director for American Management Association, he joined the Famous Artists Schools in Westport, Connecticut, where he is responsible for the design and art direction of all printed matter. In his spare time, he enjoys Fine Art painting. All of his experience has been in the visual field — the business of picture making. Many years ago, he became interested in picture framing as one method of making a good picture look even better.

Ed Reinhardt spent his early years roaming around the world as a seaman, cook and ship-rigger. During World War II he served in three branches of the service — the Merchant Marine, the Navy and the Army Air Force. In the Air Force, he ran Training Aids Departments which led to his being hired in a civilian capacity, upon discharge, to continue in research and development of visual teaching aids and methods.

"All this time," he says, "I had been fitting painting into a way of life. In 1950, I decided the cart was before the horse and since then I have devoted full time to painting."

He spent two and a half years in Florida, studying and teaching. During this time his paintings were exhibited in museums and galleries throughout the South . . . and he began to be actively interested in finding ways to make good frames inexpensively. Experimentation and experience led to the underlying principle of this book.

From Florida, Ed came north and joined the staff of the Famous Artists Schools as an instructor of painting. There, he met Hal Rogers, and the two pooled their knowledge and experience to produce this book.

The step-by-step demonstrations in this excellent do-it-yourself book are remarkably simple. Its unique format, and the ease with which it can be used as a simple "working blueprint" make it foolproof for the absolute amateur or skilled professional to produce his own fine frames. The pleasure and satisfaction of making the right frame for the right picture at no more than the cost of the raw materials, make this book a must for every artist.

Albert Dorne

President
Famous Artists Schools

Acknowledgments

For making this book possible and giving us their enthusiastic support, we wish to express our gratitude to the staff of the Famous Artists Schools and its President, Albert Dorne. To Production Manager Tom Hutson and the Photographic Department we owe a special debt for their invaluable technical advice and assistance.

Our thanks go also to:
Stanley Tools of New Britain, Conn., for their help and cooperation in choosing tools and materials.

Typography by Lettick Typografic, Inc., Bridgeport, Conn.

Photography by Zoltan Henczel

Table of Contents

Pictures – Why frame them?

By today's standards a room is not completely decorated until at least one picture is hung on the wall. The tremendous increase in the number of people studying art, the sale of prints and originals – even the popularity of the do-it-yourself picture kits – all confirm the fact that people today want pictures to live with.

What makes a good picture we leave to the taste and choice of the reader. One thing is certain, however: even an original painting worth thousands of dollars will be nothing but an eyesore if it is badly framed. On the other hand a print worth only pennies can be the source of lifelong enjoyment if it is properly framed. In short, the effect of any picture depends on the taste, proportion and craftsmanship of its frame. The right frame will enhance the presentation of any picture.

Finding the "right" frame has always been a problem. Except in the major cities, good frames are virtually unobtainable. When they are to be found, their cost is often prohibitive, even in the large cities. Whether one is a professional artist whose frame bills are a constantly recurring expense or a housewife with one print to frame, availability and cost are the two major considerations.

The simplest solution is of course to make your own frames. The raw materials are relatively inexpensive, and a frame is after all only four sticks joined together. Yet if you talk to any amateur who has tried to build a frame you will most likely encounter a long tale about the numerous pitfalls and frustrations lying in wait for the unsuspecting neophyte.

Fortunately this need not be so. This book will provide you with a thorough knowledge of how to make and finish your own picture frames simply and at moderate cost from materials which are readily available.

About this book

Before we consider the actual work, a word is necessary to those about to set up shop. A great deal of useless expense can be avoided if you define your aims first. Do you have one picture to frame? A dozen? Are you planning to make frames regularly? Read the discussions of tools, materials and moldings before you begin purchasing. You may find that you already have many of the things you need; if not, the text will provide a guide for you in finding the tools and materials which best fit your budget and degree of interest.

Throughout the book we emphasize a professional approach utilizing modern materials and methods we have found through experience to be sound. We believe that excellence need not be predicated upon complexity; therefore we have avoided the specialized formulas and cookery often associated with frame making and finishing and in their place show you practical, uncomplicated ways and means to achieve exceptional results.

The book itself is designed for your workbench rather than your bookshelf. Cross references have been kept at an absolute minimum and the convenience and usefulness further increased by grouping all the pages with construction demonstrations in the first section and all the finishing operations in the second.

Creative picture framing has a long way to go to catch up with the advances that have been made in other artistic fields. While we know that our book will give you the firm understanding of the subject needed to make good frames, we present it mainly in the hope that it will stimulate your imagination and

6

make you aware of the limitless possibilities that today's new materials and contemporary tastes bring to this traditional art.

How to begin

Good taste is always a paramount concern in framing any picture. Yet it is obvious that the most tasteful frame won't last long if it is poorly constructed. As with any undertaking, acquiring facility and skill in framing takes time and experience. Each framing problem or technique you master will give you confidence and make the next challenge that much easier to meet. The time you spend developing your craftsmanship in the early stages will be rewarded by increased skill and capability later on. Better looking, longer lasting frames take only a little longer to make than mediocre ones.

Starting on page 15, we show you how to build a frame which involves all of the fundamental construction problems you are likely to come up against. Because we all learn best by experiencing things for ourselves, we recommend that you follow the steps of the demonstration and build this first frame.

You will begin by cutting simple 90° corners in the rabbet strip. These butt joints are the easiest type to cut in a miter box. Your introduction to the 45° miter cut takes place rather painlessly on the relatively narrow insert molding. From here it is an easy step to cutting the miters in the wider drip cap molding and finally to mitering the 4 inch wide backing.

Joining and assembling operations are outlined in the same logical progression, beginning with the simplest joint and proceeding step by step to the final assembly.

In addition to gaining familiarity with your tools and confidence in your ability, you will be doubly pleased to find that the simple lines of your first frame will complement a great many paintings and drawings.

What about tools?

In setting up your shop the biggest item in your budget will be your equipment. A good deal of thought should be given to the selection of just the right tool for each job.

When you get to your hardware store and are confronted by hundreds of tools in every conceivable price range, the main factors to consider in judging which ones to buy are the use you are going to give them, the quality and the cost. It would be silly for instance to buy a $75.00 miter box to make a single frame. On the other hand, if you are going to make frames with any regularity a $2.00 miter box would be just as ridiculous a purchase. Choose the tools which best fit the program you have set for yourself.

Generally speaking, you will never go wrong choosing the tool of better quality over the cheaper one. Quality tools are more efficient, do a better job more easily and will be more economical in the long run. In addition to being less proficient, cheaper tools will need replacement more often. Read the following detailed discussions of each tool and then talk over your aims with your hardware dealer; he will be glad to help you make the best possible choice.

Workbench

The efficiency of your workbench can go a long way toward helping you do a better job more easily. It should be sturdy

No. 60

No. 115

No. 150

No. 100

enough to withstand hammering and sawing, and its surface should be level for easy frame assembly, mat cutting, glass cutting, etc. For comfort while you are working it should be about 36 inches high and large enough to accommodate any frame you are building.

Since it is easier to work around a frame than to shift the frame during construction or finishing, you will want to be able to reach your bench from all sides. Place the bench away from the wall, and if possible fasten it to the floor for added rigidity.

Because of our photographic requirements we have used a drawing table as our workbench. While we don't advise it as a permanent solution, the occasional framer might examine its possibilities as a quick means of turning a corner of the studio into a temporary frame shop.

Miter box

Together with the backsaw, the miter box is the nucleus of any framing operation. Of all the items you purchase, the biggest expenditure should be on your miter box. Absolute accuracy is mandatory — a 46° miter is not good enough; exact 45° cuts are necessary for exact 90° corners. Cheaper miter boxes can be used and in the beginning may be accurate, but with frequent use they tend to wear, wobble and become completely useless. Aside from the loss of quality, the frustration of trying to join poorly matching miters makes the original saving seem rather pointless.

In our first demonstration we have used the most inexpensive miter box and backsaw we could find to show you that a frame can be built well with extremely simple equipment. However, for a more permanently serviceable and efficient tool we recommend one of the miter boxes pictured here, or their equal. Throughout the rest of our book we have used the Stanley miter box No. 150. This medium price range tool is of excellent quality, and unless one plans to go into framing as a business it is entirely adequate for any framing job.

Backsaw

Some miter boxes are designed which can be used with an ordinary carpenter's crosscut saw; however, these saws are too flexible to use for cutting frame miters. The accuracy needed for perfectly matching miters makes the backsaw essential. This saw has a stiff "spine" which insures a truly vertical cut and avoids any twist in the completed frame.

The backsaw you buy should be the best quality you can afford. A good one will retain its set and sharpness longer and cut smoother, truer miters more quickly than a cheap one. Economizing on this tool as on the miter box is often found to be a mistake in the long run.

Choose a saw about 18 or 20 inches long, 4 to 6 inches wide, with about 12 teeth to the inch. The length enables you to cut a miter with fewer strokes, and the fine teeth produce a smooth cut which makes matching and gluing easier. These qualities produce stronger, better looking corners on your frames.

Clamps

All of the expense and effort you put into cutting accurate miters will be to no avail if, during assembly, the corners of your frames are joined carelessly.

In order to produce professional corners, you must find some means of holding the molding exactly and firmly in place while joining. The best tool for this purpose is a miter vise designed

No. 404

No. 400

expressly for the job. This specialized tool is rather expensive unless one is going to make enough frames to make it pay for itself, either in frame sales or in time saved. It does a perfect job, however, and its purchase should be considered by every serious framer.

In our search for new materials and methods we discovered a small corner clamp, tried it and found it completely adequate for moldings up to 3 inches wide. We have used it in all our demonstrations and recommend it as an economical substitute for the miter vise. Fastened to the top of your bench it is a sturdy and practical joining tool.

In addition to using this as a miter vise, you will find these clamps excellent to use when it becomes necessary to hold a frame immobile for an extended period of time. For this reason and their relatively low cost, we suggest buying four of them. They will always come in handy, even if you already own the more expensive miter vise.

You will also find a few small C clamps a worthwhile supplement to your joining tools.

Hammer
Your hammer should be chosen primarily by the way it "feels." It should be well balanced and not so heavy that it tires the wrist. Try a number of them at your hardware store and buy the one that feels best. The one we use in our demonstrations is an inexpensive tack hammer.

Pliers
A pair of combination pliers will be found very useful for removing nails and at times for driving brads into narrow moldings.

Nail set
Brads or nails are usually driven below the surface of the wood so that the holes can be filled. This prevents their discoloring the finish. A 1/16 inch nail set will be all you will need at the beginning; later on you may find a variety of sizes desirable.

Ruler
Since we have been continually reiterating the need for accuracy in framing, it is obvious that the ruler you use must be of good quality to insure exactness in all your measurements. A good straight yardstick or a six foot steel tape is imperative to good framing.

Glue
Here again one of our modern materials comes to our aid in cutting the fuss and bother of framing. Heretofore only hot cabinet glue was recommended for joining frame corners. This practice, while sound, necessitated a gluepot, heat, melting glue, smell, mess, etc. Today we can make an extremely strong joint quickly and neatly by using one of the synthetic resin glues available at any hardware counter. These glues come under a variety of trade names; all seem equally effective. They are easily recognized by their characteristic white color and pleasant odor. We recommend purchasing a one pint squeeze bottle for ease of application and economy. Larger quantities are available and are even more economical if a large number of frames are to be built.

Fasteners
Probably everyone is generally familiar with brads, nails, etc., but because picture framing is rather specialized a few words

here will make it easier for you to select the right fastener for each job.

In the main we use brads to fasten the corners of our frames. Frame moldings vary considerably in their design, so it is a good idea to have a fairly wide selection of brads on hand. This need not be a large expenditure inasmuch as brads are sold at reasonable cost in small quantities. They are graded by length and number; the number indicates their thickness. The lower the number the heavier the brad, the higher the number the thinner and finer the brad. Stick to Nos. 18 and 20 brads in lengths of 1/2 to 1 1/2 inches for the present; as you gain experience and form preferences in moldings you will find which sizes you use most often, and these can be purchased in larger quantities.

In addition to brads, on extra wide moldings skotch fasteners are used to give added strength to the corners. These are patented fasteners which are driven into the back of the frame across the miters. They pull the inside corner together and prevent gaps from forming when the brads are not long enough to do the job by themselves.

We have been examining in some detail the tools which are essential for cutting and joining frames. These tools are a must for the basic construction. As you can see, a full cabinetmaker's tool chest is not necessary; however, there are other tools you may want to acquire. For instance, while they are not absolutely mandatory, a small hand drill and a set of bits are useful to have around a frame shop. Also, as you become more interested in turning out frames of your own original design a small plane, a set of wood rasps and a few small wood chisels will be a help in modifying standard moldings.

Rather than invest a large sum at the outset, we recommend that these and similar supplementary tools be bought as they are needed to make specific jobs easier.

At the beginning of each demonstration you will find a photograph, list and description of all the tools and materials needed for that particular operation. To the left is a general list for quick reference:

Construction:

Miter box
Backsaw
Ruler
Clamps
Hammer
Pliers
Nail set

Covering Inserts — Mats:

Scissors
X-acto knife

Mat Cutting:

Mat knife
Oilstone
Compass

Finishing:

Brushes
Paint scraper
Rasp
Comb

Glass Cutting:

Glass cutter
Straightedge

Gilding:

Gilder's tip

Mounting Prints:

Roller
Brushes

Assembly:

Ice pick

What about moldings?

Broadly speaking, there are two types of molding available to the framer: picture frame molding and builder's molding. The former is designed exclusively for use in picture framing while the latter is used for the trim in home building.

The major technical difference between the two is that picture frame molding has a rabbet cut into it. This feature makes building a frame a little simpler; however, it is difficult for the individual to buy picture frame molding unless he has access to a large city supply center. Even then it is often necessary to buy a relatively large quantity of a single profile in order to bring the price per foot within reason. Furthermore, unless one is very familiar with molding profiles, they can be difficult to visualize and disappointments can result when buying by mail. For these reasons we took a long look at what builder's molding had to offer the framer.

First of all we found that builder's moldings come in an amazingly wide range of profiles and sizes. A great many of them make suitable picture frame moldings "as is," while a still greater number work excellently when combined with others. The over 50 frame variations we show you how to make in this book were designed using only 8 common profiles. The possibilities are unlimited; with a little thought the "right" frame can be designed for any picture.

Some moldings are thick enough to have a rabbet cut directly into them; your lumber yard will do this for you at the time of your purchase, otherwise the rabbet can be made very simply by adding a strip of wood to the back of the molding. We use a standard 1/2 x 3/4 inch parting strip for this purpose. On these grounds, and because they are so inexpensive and easy for everyone to obtain, we have used builder's moldings for all our demonstrations. It should be kept in mind, however, that the principles of framing which we discuss will apply to any type of molding.

Moldings of course are the heart of picture framing; the effectiveness of any frame rests primarily on the design and proportion of its molding. Finding the right molding can be fun when you have some idea of what to look for.

Choosing your molding

Setting forth any set rules about which molding to choose for any given picture is always rather difficult. Tastes and trends in framing are continually changing and what is "the way" to frame a watercolor, for instance, today may be out of style in a relatively short time. Therefore, the following are given only as rather general characteristics of how various types of pictures are framed today. It is hoped the reader will feel free and stimulated to bring his own innovations to any framing project. In this way picture framing will be kept an alive and exciting art.

Oil paintings are always framed without glass. The moldings found most suitable are generally fairly wide and deep, although this is not necessarily always true. Conventional or academic subjects usually look well in frames 4 to 6 inches wide, while a simple, thin strip frame is all that is required for some of the more abstract pictures.

To make the transition from picture to frame smooth and harmonious, an insert or liner will often be found desirable. In fact, the use of an insert should always be considered when framing any oil painting.

Original black and white prints and drawings are usually framed under glass with a white or off-white mat. The molding is generally rather narrow and either natural wood or black.

Original color prints are framed in the same way although, having the added virtue of color, they permit more originality in the use of color in the mat and frame.

Watercolors are always framed under glass and are usually matted in either white, gray or a color which enhances the painting. Watercolor frames have become more and more experimental and creative of late. Perhaps this is an effort on the part of the artist to destroy the "little medium" tag that has been applied to watercolor for so many years and give the work equal status with oil painting. At any rate the trend is a welcome one.

Prints and reproductions of oils, watercolors, etc., are best framed to resemble the original medium.

Since the designs of builder's moldings are based on function, they are fairly standard. You may find, however, that the style or pattern of the decoration used will vary slightly in different sections of the country. At your lumber yard you will find a chart similar to the one shown here. From it you can get an idea of the stock your dealer has available. Then go right to the molding racks and browse. Not only will you have fun poking around, but you will find that seeing the actual moldings will help to gen-

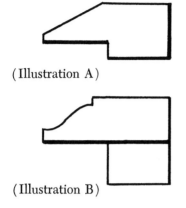

(Illustration A)

(Illustration B)

erate ideas for frame designs. Very often a cross section on a chart will not be as visually effective as the molding itself.

Sometimes the exact profile you have in mind will not be obtainable and a compromise becomes necessary. By actually having the moldings at hand the closest likeness can be found.

The molding we use for our insert is a good example of such a compromise. The profile we were looking for was something like illustration A (left).

The nearest thing we could find was a 1 3/4 inch molded stop of a style popular in this locale. It has a silhouette like illustration B (left).

We could see immediately that with the addition of a parting strip rabbet it would do the job excellently.

When you decide on a molding, pick over the supply for the best strips. Check for warpage by sighting down each strip. Choose strips which are free of knots and have no excess sap or bark areas. It is important also to check that the molding profile has not been broken down or worn in handling. The little extra effort it takes to go through a pile of molding will be repaid with less waste and better looking finished frames.

Moldings are sold in even foot lengths: 6, 8, 10, 12 and 14 feet. You can easily find how much molding to purchase for each frame by adding the lengths of the four sides of your picture and eight times the width of the molding. This allowance is one which beginners are apt to forget; remember, the miters will add length to each side of the frame.

As an example let's assume we are going to buy enough 2 inch molding to frame a 16 x 20 inch picture. By adding: 16 + 16 + 20 + 20 + 16 (the width allowance), we can see that we will need 7 feet 4 inches of molding. A little excess is better than not enough, so we would buy an 8 foot strip of the molding. The short scraps left over from strips like this make excellent test pieces upon which to try finishes, or they may be built into sample corners.

After a few excursions among the stacks of lumber at your dealer's, you will become quite adept at finding the correct profile molding for all of your pictures.

General notes on moldings

1 — The design of the molding you choose must relate to the picture you are framing.

2 — A traditional painting looks best in a frame with a familiar, timeworn (traditional) feeling.

3 — A positive, bold painting demands a frame with strong, simple lines.

4 — Light, airy compositions should be surrounded with a frame of comparable delicacy.

5 — A picture whose paint quality has a distinctly textural feeling is complemented by a frame rich in texture.

6 — Modern two-dimensional pictures are best framed with moldings which are either flat in profile or recede towards the wall.

7 — Compositions which employ traditional perspective are further enhanced by a molding design which is fairly deep and slants in toward the picture.

12

What about finishing?

The second half of our book is devoted to the various ways you can finish picture frames. The subject of finishing is an important one, because in the final analysis the success or failure of a picture's presentation will depend upon the finish of its frame.

The finishing demonstrations start on page 72. In this section we demonstrate toning, texturing, gilding, glass cutting, mat cuttings, covering mats and inserts, mounting prints, refinishing antique frames and wiring pictures for hanging.

Each demonstration treats in detail the tools and materials used for that particular operation; however, before you start a few brief comments on the aims of finishing and on some of the specialized materials used are in order.

In this phase of picture framing, as with construction, we experimented with new materials and methods. For each operation, we present the simplest and least involved way for you to achieve professional looking finishes.

A good finish must not clash with the picture; therefore, as a general rule, any finish you use should be rather neutral in character. Depending on the qualities of the picture, a warm or cool gray tone will be found most suitable. While the grayness can be modified slightly to fit special traits, remember that in a frame finish a slight leaning towards neutrality is much preferred to a too dark or intense color.

The most exciting and useful new finishing materials we found are the new, extra thick "no-drip" paints, now available for home decorating. These paints can be purchased in any paint store under a variety of trade names. They usually have a plastic or vinyl base and are water soluble. For simplicity we will refer to the paint we use throughout the rest of the book as "vinyl base paint."

The paints are usually mixed to a heavy consistency and come in many colors. For frame finishing purposes you need buy only white. Its extra thickness allows it to be used undiluted as a means of texturing your frames. Tinted with inexpensive colorants and thinned with water, it will also make excellent toning washes called *patinas*.

Patinas

To avoid harshness and insure a pleasingly soft tone in your patinas, it is always advisable to start with a basic gray and modify it to suit the particular picture you are framing. You could start each patina right from the white, but this takes longer than is necessary and is apt to result in colors which are too strong and overpowering.

On page 73 we show you how to mix a basic palette of finishing patinas. We use the thick white paint, raw umber and black to arrive at a neutral gray patina which provides the base for any further mixing.

Glazing

This process, as its name implies, consists of wiping a thin, transparent wash of color over a frame. While a glaze takes comparatively longer to dry than a patina, it is sometimes useful in making fine adjustments of tone over a patinized frame or as a means of darkening natural wood moldings.

Almost any color can be used when glazing. As in any finishing operation, however, neutrality and harmony should be sought.

The quickest and simplest way to glaze a frame is to dip a

large pad of cloth into a thin mixture of oil color and turpentine and wipe it quickly across the surface to be toned. If the tone is too dark it can easily be lightened by rubbing very lightly with fine steel wool.

Gilding

This traditional art has long been the "Cadillac" of finishing operations. Whole books have been justifiably devoted to this subject alone. Skill in handling the fickle leaf takes years to acquire, and the amateur has always been warned against trying the rather ticklish procedure. Even if he did finally make a good gild, was the amount of time it took worth it?

We believe gilding is fun, so we set about finding ways which would encourage even beginning finishers to try it.

It is always advisable to apply metal leaf to a smooth surface. Preparing the ground can become an art in itself. The ground is usually made of gilder's clay, which can be finished to a glass-like smoothness.

Our heavy-bodied white paint again proved to be the solution to a knotty problem. We found that by coating the area to be gilded with this paint undiluted and steel wooling each coat, any degree of smoothness could be arrived at quickly and simply.

Of course, achieving expertness in handling the leaf will still take time, but the three gilding methods we show you will, we hope, stimulate you to explore further this facet of finishing.

Mounting prints

A print, map, photograph or drawing is fastened to a heavier backing in order to give it more substance and permanence. The procedure is a simple one which you should have no difficulty in following.

The prime factor in mounting any picture is the adhesive used. It should have good holding power, be clean and easy to use and not create excess warpage when it dries.

There are many adhesives on the market, but the one we use in our demonstration has all these qualities and is also water soluble, which makes brush cleaning easy. It dries smoothly and quickly under light pressure.

Now to work

Utilizing the benefits of contemporary ideas and materials does not imply a desire to produce novelty at any cost. Ideally a picture frame should combine the best of the traditions of the past, the tastes of the present and the visions of the future. The wide range and flexibility of today's materials provide the means with which the framer can free his mind from thoughts of chemistry and fuss and concentrate his energies on the really creative aspects of his art.

We must always remember that a picture frame, no matter how creative or original, does not exist for itself. It should be conceived as an integral part of the living space in which it is seen. The framer's job is to create a visual bridge or stepping stone between the picture and its environment, which invites the viewer to visit the world contained within.

Simplicity is the key word in our presentation, and the modern framer, when faced with the choice of which molding or finish to use on a particular picture, will not go wrong if he will keep this word foremost.

A frame is after all four simple sticks . . .

The basic insert

The basic insert we show you how to make consists of two wooden rectangles, one of which is fastened to the back of the other. The rectangle in front is the face of the insert; the rectangle in back forms the rabbet to hold the picture.

For the face of the insert we use 1⅜ inch molded stop. The rabbet is made from ½ x ¾ inch parting strip.

We start by building the rectangle which goes next to our picture and forms the rabbet.

Tools — Miter box, backsaw, C clamps, framing clamp, hammer, yardstick, pencil.

Materials — One 8 foot piece molded stop, one 8 foot piece parting strip, ¾ and 1¼ inch brads, glue.

molded stop

parting strip

actual size

1 Measuring — We cut about ¼ inch from one end of the parting strip to square it. We then mark it 16⅛ inches from the squared end. The ⅛ inch is added to any picture measurement to allow some play for easier fitting.

2 Cutting — When the rabbet strip does not show in the finished frame there is no need to miter the corners; we can make it stronger using simple butt joints. Holding the strip firmly in the miter box we make the first 90° cut at the 16⅛ inch mark. Keep the saw as close to horizontal as possible.

3 Measuring — Using the first piece as a pattern we mark the second short side. It is important to use the first piece as a pattern to ensure getting both pieces exactly the same length.

4 **Cutting** — Now we are making the second 90° cut.

5 **Cutting** — Here we are making the final cut, the two shorter sides have been made and we repeated steps 1, 2 and 3 to make the longer ones. In measuring the long sides allow ⅛ inch for play and an additional 1½ inches for the overlap needed to make the butt joint. These strips will be 21⅝ inches long.

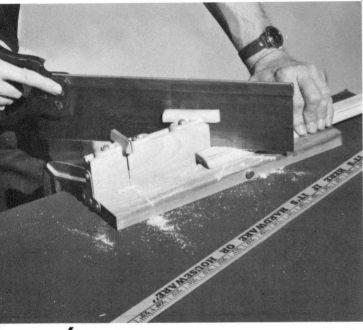

6 **Cutting** — With the rabbet strip cut we make the first 45° miter near the end of the molded stop. Be sure the angle is in the right direction; the slanted edge of the wood will go inside next to the picture.

7 **Measuring** — Mitered pieces will normally be measured on the inside or short edge of the molding. However, when we assemble the insert, the square edge of the molded stop has to match the outside edge of the rabbet strip; therefore we are measuring 21⅝ inches along the outside edge.

8 **Cutting** — Having cut the first long side, we now cut the first miter on the second side.

9 **Measuring** — With the end of the remaining stock mitered we are using the first side as a pattern to mark the second long side.

10 Measuring — After cutting the two long sides we again mark the outside edge of the molding, this time for the first short side. Make this piece 17⅝ inches.

11 Cutting — Now we use the first short side as a pattern — then cut our final miter. With this operation the cutting of the insert is complete.

Cutting completed — The four pieces of molding for the face of the insert and the four pieces of parting strip, which will form the rabbet, are now cut and ready to assemble.

12 Gluing — Choosing one long and one short side of the parting strip, we apply glue to one end of the shorter piece. Cover the surface fully.

13 Clamping — Here the two pieces have been placed together and locked in the framing clamp ready for nailing. The long side covers the end of the short one as shown. Make sure the strips are flat against the bottom and sides of the clamp. Tighten each side gradually; the clamp will then bring the surfaces evenly and firmly together.

14 Nailing — We use two 1½ inch #20 brads in each corner. With the clamp as tight as possible the first brad is driven in near the outside edge.

15 Nailing — For added insurance against twisting, the second brad is placed near the inside edge of the strip, slightly lower than the first.

16 Nailing — One half of the rabbet is now done. We go through the same operations with the second half, making sure the long piece overlaps the short one.

17 Nailing — The same gluing and nailing steps are used to join the two halves into the finished rabbet strip.

18 Gluing — With the rabbet strip completed we begin to assemble the face of the insert. We apply glue evenly to the mitered surfaces of the molded stop.

19 Clamping — The glued ends of one long and one short side of molded stop are placed in the clamp. Tighten each side of the framing clamp gradually, pulling the miters together at the inside corner. The edges should match.

20 Nailing — Drive two brads in this corner; place one of them as close as possible to the inside edge of the molding to help prevent twisting the frame.

21 Nailing — Three of the corners have been joined and the final brad is being driven home. A small block of scrap wood under the previously assembled corners keeps the halves level and assures a "flat" frame.

Ready to assemble — The face and the rabbet strip are both completed and ready to be joined.

22 Gluing — Covering one entire surface of the rabbet strip with glue prepares it for joining.

23 Nailing — The glued surface of the rabbet strip is placed on the back of the molding with the outside edges carefully matched. Some ¾ inch brads, our hammer — and the insert is complete.

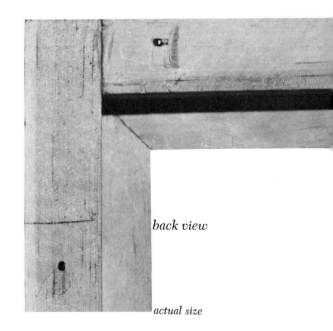

back view

actual size

The completed insert

1 x 4 flat

The frame we show you how to build here is never used by itself. However, in combination with other moldings and inserts it provides the basis for an astonishing variety of excellent frames. It is simple to build and you should have no trouble following the step by step demonstration — and, incidentally, picking up some excellent experience which will help later on when you tackle more complicated moldings.

Tools — Miter box, backsaw, C clamps, hammer, yardstick, pencil, square.

Materials — One 10 foot piece 1 x 4 clear pine, 6d finishing nails, skotch fasteners, glue.

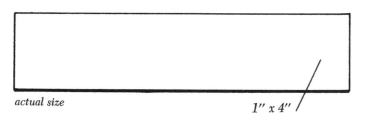

actual size   1" x 4"

1 **Cutting** — From one end of our stock we cut our first 45° miter. Make sure the 1 x 4 is held firmly and *flat* against the bottom and back of the miter box.

2 **Measuring** — We use the completed insert as a guide to measure the first short side. Allow about 1/16 inch extra here for easier fitting.

3 Cutting — Making sure the miter is going in the right direction, we cut the first piece of our frame.

4 Measuring — No need to trim off the end again — with a flat board like this just match the first piece to the mitered end, mark carefully and we're ready to cut the other short side.

5 Cutting — Now the two short sides are finished. We have measured one long side against the insert — again allowing 1/16 inch for play — cut it, and use it to mark the final piece which we are cutting here.

Cutting completed — The frame is now cut and the four sides are ready to be joined.

6 Gluing — We coat the mitered end of one of the short sides fully and evenly.

7 Clamping — Our framing clamp will not take a molding this wide, so we are using C clamps to hold the wood against the flat surface of the table. Small pieces of scrap wood are used under the clamps to prevent scarring the surface. The corner must make an exact 90° angle, so we check the inside edge with our square. With the clamps almost tight you can adjust the angle of the corner exactly with light taps of your hammer. Make sure the miters are firmly together — tighten the clamps and your corner is ready for nailing.

8 Nailing — In this step we have driven a skotch fastener across the miter, and are pulling the outside edges together with 6d finishing nails. When these nails have been driven in we will further strengthen the corner with another skotch fastener.

½ actual size

The completed frame

9 Setting — Since the corners of this frame will be seen we are setting the nails. Place the nail set on each nailhead and tap lightly until the nailhead is well below the surface of the wood. The holes will later be filled with wood dough. You will find this operation easier to perform holding the finished frame vertically on the floor.

Drip cap no. 1

Drip cap for the frame maker is one of the most versatile moldings to be found in the lumber yard. Here is the first of many handsome picture frames you can build from this simple molding.

drip cap

actual size

Tools — Miter box, backsaw, C clamps, yardstick, framing clamp, hammer, nail set.

Materials — One 8 foot piece drip cap molding, basic insert, glue, 1½ inch brads.

1 Cutting — We start by holding the drip cap firmly against the bottom and back of the miter box and make the first 45° cut, near the end of the strip. Be sure the miter cut is made in the right direction — for this frame the shorter, thinner edge of the drip cap will go next to the insert.

2 Measuring — Now we measure the first long side of our frame — 20⅝ inches *along the inside edge*. This will allow about ⅝ inch of the insert to show next to the picture.

3 **Cutting** — Having made the cut that completes the first long side, we now start our first cut on the second long side.

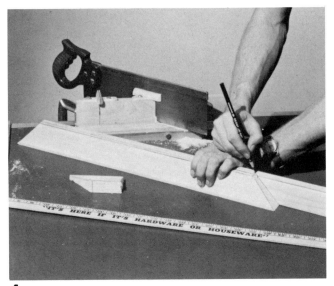

4 **Measuring** — Using the first side as a pattern, we mark the length on the uncut end of the second piece, and make the cut which completes the two long sides.

5 **Cutting** — Here two long sides and one short side have been completed. We are cutting the second short side, which measures 16⅝ inches on the inside edge, again allowing ⅝ inch of insert exposed.

Cutting completed — The four pieces of drip cap molding have been cut and are ready for assembly.

6 Gluing — Choosing one short and one long piece of drip cap we apply glue evenly to the cut surfaces.

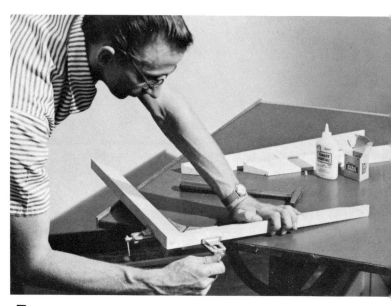

7 Clamping — Here the two glued surfaces have been fitted together and are being locked in the framing clamp for nailing. Keep any discrepancy in the sizes of the two pieces on the outside. This "overhang" can be sanded off later. (See drawing.)

Outside overhang can be sanded off later.

8 Nailing — With the clamp tightened we nail the first half together with two 1½ inch brads. To prevent twisting we space them as shown in the drawing below.

9 Nailing — Here we nail the other side of the corner. If glue oozes out while you nail, wipe it off.

10 Nailing — One half of the frame is done, so we go through the same joining operation with the second half.

11 Joining — With each half of the frame assembled, we now glue and nail the two halves together.

12 Setting — Holding the frame in a vertical position we set the nails. We use the framing clamp in each corner as an extra precaution against springing the joints.

3/4 actual size

The completed frame

Assembly

Here is where careful workmanship pays off. If our three rectangles — insert, 1 x 4 and drip cap — are accurate we will shortly have our first frame completed, ready for finishing.

Tools — Hammer, pliers.
Materials — Glue, 1¼ inch nails.

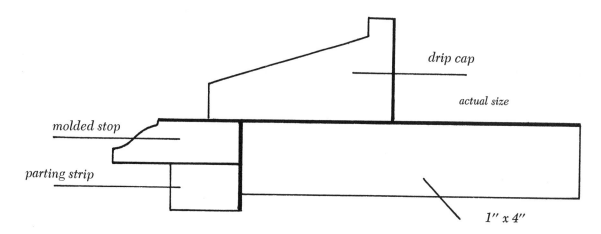

drip cap

actual size

molded stop

parting strip

1" x 4"

1 Gluing — Squeezing glue over the entire back surface of the drip cap rectangle prepares it for joining.

2 Temporary nailing — With the 1 x 4 rectangle face up (skotch fasteners down), we center the drip cap equidistant from the outer edges, making sure the miter cuts match at the corners. We toenail (drive a brad at an angle) through each side of the drip cap *part way* into the 1 x 4 beneath.

3 Permanent nailing — Turning the frame over we drive 1¼ inch brads through the 1 x 4 into the drip cap underneath. Three brads in each side will hold. Now for the insert . . .

4 Installing the insert — We drop the insert face down into the opening in the back of the 1 x 4 rectangle — against the drip cap. We toenail 1¼ inch nails *part* way into each side through the back of the insert into the 1 x 4. No glue and only four nails are used here, as the insert should be removable.

Flip the frame over — withdraw the two temporary nails from the front of the frame and you have . . .

2/3 actual size

The completed frame

Drip cap no. 2

Here is a striking reverse frame, completely different in character from the first frame we showed you how to build. It is made from the same moldings, an 8 foot piece of drip cap molding and a basic insert. We used the 16 x 20 inch insert we showed you how to build on pages 15 through 20.

Tools — Miter box, backsaw, C clamps, yardstick, framing clamp, hammer, 1½ inch brads.

Materials — One 8 foot piece drip cap molding, basic insert, glue, 1½ inch brads.

drip cap

actual size

1 Cutting — With the drip cap molding held firmly in the miter box we trim off the end of the stock, making our first 45° miter. Notice the position of the molding — for this frame design the drip cap is held in a vertical position.

2 Measuring — We now hold the mitered end against the edge of the insert and mark the first long side of our frame. Make this measurement very carefully — the molding when assembled must fit exactly around the insert.

4 Measuring — We swung the saw and cut the first miter on the second side — duplicating step one. Then matching the two mitered ends we use the first side as a pattern to measure for the second miter.

3 Cutting — Holding our drip cap in the same position as in the first step we swing the saw of our miter box to the opposite 45° angle and make the second cut, completing the first long side of our frame.

5 Cutting — Now we place the molding in the miter box in the same position, swing our saw and cut the second long side.

6 Cutting — We have followed the same measuring and cutting operations and are now making the final miter on the second piece.

Cutting completed — Ready for joining — compare these 4 pieces with those of Frame Number One; see how turning the drip cap makes the same molding completely different in design.

7 Gluing — Apply a liberal coating of glue to the miters of one long and one short side.

8 Nailing — We carefully clamp the corners and drive two 1½ inch brads into one side and one into the other. To avoid scarring the frame we don't drive the brads all the way in.

Nailing detail — Here is a close-up of all three brads in place. Notice that the heads are still above the surface of the wood.

9 Setting — By setting the brads we will have only three small holes to fill.

10 Nailing — Here the second half of our frame is in the clamp and the final brad is being driven in. Set these brads and the two halves are ready to be joined.

11 Joining — With three of the corners glued and nailed, we are now nailing the final one. We use small scraps of parting strip under each corner to keep the frame level and untwisted.

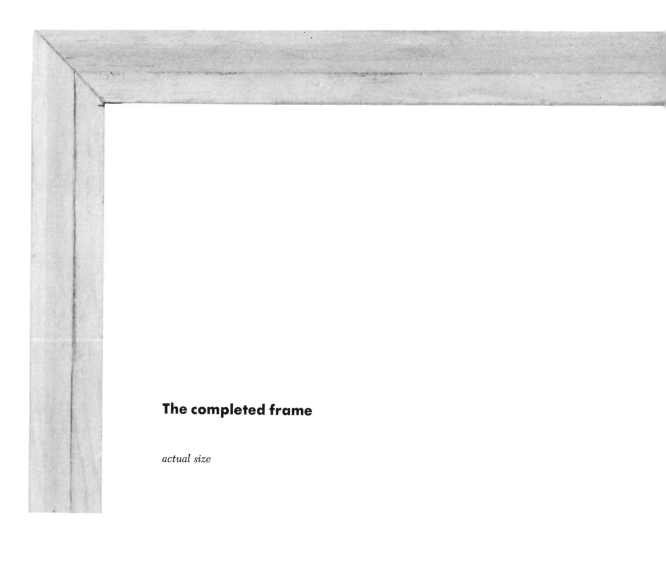

The completed frame

actual size

Assembly

The reverse drip cap frame we have just shown you how to build can be easily combined with the basic insert to make a molding design which has the quality of giving a picture more substance. It works especially well with pictures which rely on their two-dimensional design for impact.

Tools — Hammer.

Materials — Insert, glue, 1 inch brads.

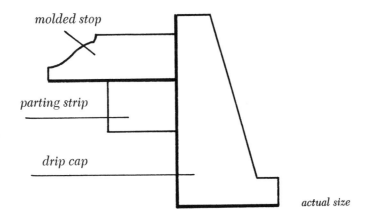

molded stop

parting strip

drip cap

actual size

1 Ready to assemble — Our frame is completed, and, if we have measured carefully, ready to be joined with the insert.

2 Gluing — We have tried our insert — it fits perfectly — so we apply glue all around the flat outside edge.

3 Positioning insert — Holding the frame vertically makes it simple to slide the insert in from the back. Any excess glue which squeezes out will then be on the back where it can't spoil the looks of our frame.

4 Positioning detail — To make sure our insert is in the right position we line up its top edge with the bottom edge of the groove on the inside of the drip cap.

5 Nailing — With the frame still held vertically and the insert in position we nail through the rabbet strip, fastening the insert to the drip cap.

This shot is a good demonstration of why we slide the insert in from the back of the frame in step number 3. The slight irregularities apparent on the inside edge of the drip cap are the small beads of excess glue squeezed out by the tight fit. They would be most unwelcome on the front edge.

The completed frame

actual size

Variations

36

Clamshell no. 1

On the next few pages we will show you how a molding normally used for interior trim can be made into a handsome modern frame. You'll find that clamshell molding, plus the basic insert, makes a design which will complement most pictures.

Tools — Miter box, backsaw, hammer, C clamps, square.

Materials — The basic insert, one 10 foot piece clamshell (wide), scotch fasteners, brads, glue.

actual size

clamshell

1 Cutting — We start by cutting a miter on one end of our molding — for this frame design, the square end of the clamshell is held against the back of the miter box.

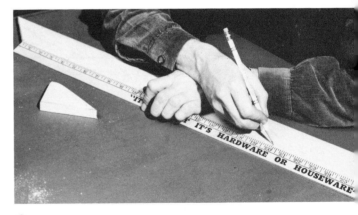

2 Measuring — We mark our long picture dimension plus ⅛ inch for play along the square inside edge of the molding.

3 Cutting — With the saw swung to the opposite 45° angle and the clamshell held firmly, we cut the first long side.

4 Measuring — We have repeated step one and are using the first piece as a pattern to measure the second long side.

Cutting completed — The four pieces of clamshell molding have been cut and are ready to be joined.

5 Cutting — Following the same measuring procedure for our short sides, we are here cutting the last miter.

6 Gluing — With one long side clamped face down to the table with a C clamp, we spread glue on the end of one short side. A piece of scrap wood under the clamp prevents marring the surface.

7 Clamping — We check the corner for squareness, tighten the clamps firmly and the corner is ready for fastening.

9 Nailing — After putting a second skotch fastener in place we drive a brad into one side to keep the thin edges of our molding together.

8 Fastening — We drive one skotch fastener across the miter.

10 Joining — We have repeated steps 8 and 9, completing the second half of our frame. With this fourth corner fastened our joining is finished.

11 Drying — Clamping the frame face up on the bench, allow the glue about an hour to set hard. A piece of 1 x 4 under the clamps distributes the pressure evenly and holds the frame flat.

The completed frame

2/3 actual size

Assembly

Follow these four easy steps and you can combine the clamshell frame you have just finished with a basic insert to create this distinctive silhouette.

As you can see the insert is fastened to the face of the clamshell; therefore it is important to miter the corners of the rabbet strip instead of using the butt joints demonstrated earlier.

Tools — C clamps, hammer, insert.

Materials — One inch brads, glue, clamshell frame, the basic insert.

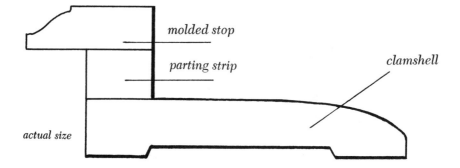

molded stop

parting strip

clamshell

actual size

Ready to assemble

1 Gluing — We spread an even coat of glue over the back of the insert.

2 Temporary nailing — The clamshell frame is placed face down on the glued surface of the insert, and its inside corners are lined up with the corners of the rabbet strip. We then drive a brad through each side of the clamshell part way into the insert.

3 Checking — The corners are checked from the front to see that the miters match, and the frame is ready to be permanently fastened.

4 Permanent nailing — With the frame again face down we are using one inch brads to finish our assembly. Place the brads about four inches apart around the entire frame.

actual size

The completed frame

Clamshell no. 2

The narrow clamshell molding we use for this frame is the same design as the wide clamshell used in the preceding demonstration. Turning it on end and adding the basic insert creates a reverse frame of excellent proportions.

Tools — Miter box, backsaw, hammer, framing clamp, nail set.

Materials — The basic insert, one 10 foot piece clamshell (narrow) 1¼ inch brads, glue.

clamshell

actual size

2 Measuring — We then use the insert as a pattern to mark the length of the first long side.

1 Cutting — Holding the clamshell vertically against the back of the miter box, we make the first miter cut.

3 Cutting — Here we cut the second miter, completing the first long side.

4 Measuring — After repeating step one, the first long side serves as a pattern to mark the second.

5 Cutting — Here we are making the cut that completes the second long side.

6 Cutting — Again using the insert as a guide we have marked and cut the first short side of our frame. This final miter on the second short side completes the frame.

Cutting completed

7 Gluing — Taking one short and one long side we spread glue on the cut ends before placing them into the clamp.

8 Clamping and nailing — With the clamshell tight in our clamp we drive the first 1¼ inch brad into one side near the top edge. (Don't drive the brads in all the way.)

9 Setting — After driving two brads into each side we use our nail set to drive the brad heads beneath the surface, completing one half of our frame.

10 Joining — We repeated step nine on the other half of our frame and are now joining the two halves in the same manner. Note blocks supporting the unclamped corners of frame.

The completed frame   *actual size*

Assembly

A basic insert, the vertical clamshell frame and these four easy assembly steps will give you a molding whose silhouette will work especially well with the more contemporary paintings.

Tools — Hammer.

Materials — Basic insert, vertical clamshell frame, 1 inch brads, glue.

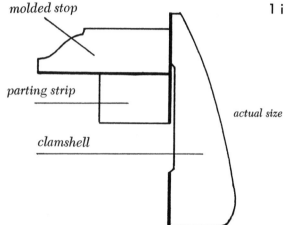

molded stop

parting strip

clamshell

actual size

1 Marking — A pencil line about ¼ inch inside the edge of the clamshell will guide us in positioning the insert.

Ready to assemble — After trying the insert to make sure it fits inside the clamshell, we are ready to assemble the moldings. In this particular case our small plane was needed to trim the insert, which was a little too tight.

2 Gluing — We coat the edges of the insert fully and evenly with glue.

3 Positioning — Working from the back we bring the insert up to the pencil lines.

4 Nailing — In the center of each side we drive a brad through the clamshell part way into the insert — check the position; then brads about every four inches will hold.

The completed frame

actual size

Variations

47

Scoop cove

A simple scoop is perhaps the most widely used frame molding profile. The builder's molding that most closely resembles this classic silhouette is called sprung cove. While it is a little tricky to handle because it has no large flat areas to keep it true in the miter box, the simple jig we show you here will enable you to cut exact miters when you have a picture which calls for this popular frame design.

Tools — Miter box, backsaw, hammer, C clamps, square.

Materials — One 8 foot piece of sprung cove molding, glue, brads, basic insert.

cove molding

actual size

Jig set up — Two pieces of parting strip clamped to the miter box will keep the molding flat against the bottom and back of the miter box.

1 Cutting — We trim the end off our stock. In cutting this molding, the edge on the bottom of the miter box will be the edge which goes next to the picture. You can see how the strips of wood keep the molding in position, assuring a true miter.

Close-up

2 Positioning – To locate the cove molding on the insert, the flat bottom of the cove is aligned with the outside edge of the insert. We then mark all four corners in the same way. With the molding held in position we mark the length of the first long side.

3 Cutting – We swing our saw to the opposite 45° angle and miter the other end of the first long side.

4 Cutting – Now we trim the end off our remaining stock – the first cut on the second long side.

5 **Measuring** — Using the first long side as a pattern, we mark the second long side.

6 **Cutting** — We completed the two long sides and repeated the same steps on the short sides. Here we are making the final cut on the second short side.

Cutting completed— The four sides of our frame are cut and we are now ready to tackle the tricky job of joining.

7 **Gluing and clamping** — Choosing one long and one short side we spread glue evenly over the mitered surfaces. We have inserted our molding in the framing clamp upside down to take advantage of the flat surface of the molding and also to bring our nailing surface up where we can see it.

8 **Nailing** — After driving two brads into one side of the corner we now drive two more into the other. In this close-up you can see that the brads are not driven all the way in.

9 **Setting** — To complete this corner our nail set is used to sink the brad heads below the surface.

10 **Joining** — After repeating steps 7, 8 and 9 with the other corners of our frame, we are now driving the last brad in the final corner.

2/3 actual size

The completed frame

Assembly

Of all the frames we show you how to make this particular combination of cove molding and an insert would probably come closest to being what is popularly thought of as a "frame."

Tools — Hammer.

Materials — Scoop cove frame, a basic insert, glue, 1 inch brads.

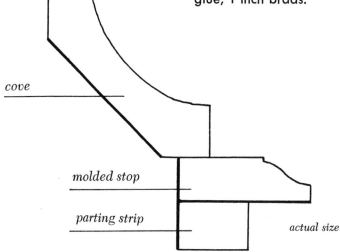

cove

molded stop

parting strip

actual size

Ready to assemble — The basic insert and our frame are ready to be fastened together. The frame is shown with the back facing up.

1 Gluing — We spread an even coat of glue along the entire back edge of the frame.

2 Positioning — After lining up the outside edge of the insert with the edge of the cove we hold the insert in place and turn the frame over. We check to make sure the insert is positioned evenly within the frame before nailing it in place.

3 Nailing — Turning the frame so that the back is again up, we drive 1 inch brads through the insert into the cove — about four to a side will do the job.

The completed frame

2/3 actual size

53

Reverse cove

With sprung cove molding and the same jig we used in the previous demonstration we can create an up-to-date frame with a classic flavor. This frame has all the good features of a modern reverse frame, and at the same time the character of the curved molding softens any severity. You'll find this design will work surprisingly well with a wide variety of pictures.

Tools — Miter box, backsaw, hammer, C clamps, nail set.

Materials — One 8 foot piece sprung cove molding, glue, brads, a basic insert.

cove

actual size

1 Cutting — First we trim one end of our stock — note that in this case the edge against the back of the miter box is the one that goes next to the picture.

Jig set up

2 Measuring — Using the insert as a pattern we mark the first long side. Make this measurement very carefully — it is important that the molding fit around the insert exactly.

3 Cutting — We miter the marked end which completes the first long side.

4 Cutting — With the first side cut we trim the end of our remaining stock.

6 Cutting — After completing the second long side we repeat the same steps to make the short sides. Here the final cut is being made.

5 Measuring — Using the first long side as a pattern we mark the second long side.

Cutting completed

7 Gluing and clamping — Clamping one long side to the table, we apply glue to the end of a short piece. We then bring the two miters together and place a clamp on the short side; after checking the corner for squareness we tighten the clamps. Use a piece of wood under the clamps to protect the molding, and keep the clamps close to the edge to avoid twisting the frame. This is tricky — it took us two tries.

8 Nailing — Success — with both pieces clamped firmly in place we drive one brad into one side and two into the other. Don't try to drive the brads all the way in; you may scar your frame.

10 Joining — Repeating the same operation on the opposite half, we are now joining the final corner.

9 Setting — Using our nail set we sink the brad heads below the surface of the wood — this completes one half.

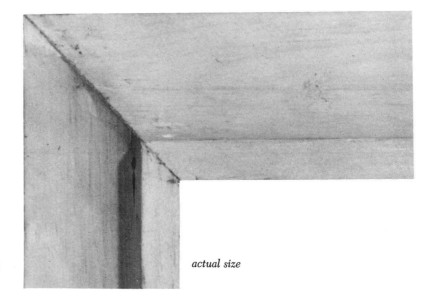

The completed frame

actual size

Assembly

A hammer, a few brads and some glue are all you need to combine the reverse cove frame with a basic insert. In checking our insert with the frame we found the insert a little big — it happens to all of us at times, and in this case a little had to be planed off one side of the insert.

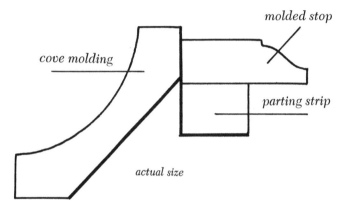

cove molding

molded stop

parting strip

actual size

1 Gluing — We spread glue evenly on the surfaces to be joined.

2 Nailing — We position the insert about ¼ inch in from the top of the frame and drive brads in from the outside. Use the nail set for the final blows.

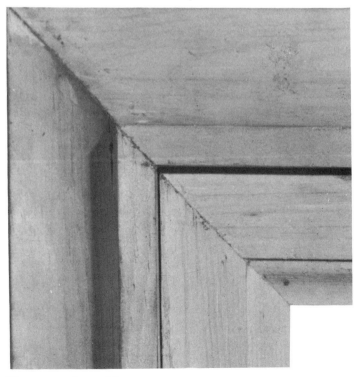

The completed frame   *actual size*

Variations

Nose cove

Up to this point we have shown you numerous ways to adapt standard moldings to create tasteful picture frames. We have turned them, stood them on end and used them in various combinations. An additional way to utilize ordinary moldings is to cut a rabbet in one edge. For this demonstration we are using nose cove molding with a rabbet cut in the square edge. With a little experimentation you will find others which will also work with a rabbet.

If you own a power saw, you can cut the rabbet yourself; if not, your lumber yard will cut it for you. Take your book along and refer them to step one.

Tools — Miter box, backsaw, hammer, framing clamp.

Materials — One 8 foot piece nose cove molding, glue, 1½ inch 20 gauge brads.

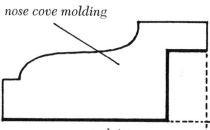

nose cove molding

actual size

1 Cutting the rabbet — First set your saw to make a ¾ inch deep cut; then with the guide set ¼ inch from the blade, hold the molding horizontally and run it through. WATCH YOUR FINGERS — the rabbet should be in the *molding*. To complete the rabbet, set the saw for a ¼ inch deep cut and the guide ¾ inch from the blade. Hold the molding as shown and make the cut.

2 Cutting — With the rabbeted edge of the molding against the back of the miter box we cut our first 45° miter near one end.

3 Measuring — Because we are not able to see the rabbet when we cut this molding, a little figuring is necessary to measure the length of the sides. Here is the procedure to follow: Picture measurement + ⅛ inch − ½ inch. For example, our first side is 20 inches, plus ⅛ inch for play, minus ¼ inch at each end for our rabbet, thus we mark 19⅝ inches on the inside edge of our molding.

4 Cutting — After swinging our saw to the opposite 45° position, and secure in the knowledge that we have measured correctly, we cut our second miter, completing the first long side of our frame.

5 Measuring — We have cut off the end of the remaining stock, and, using the first side as a pattern, we are now marking the length of the second long side.

6 Cutting — Following the same measuring procedure on the short sides — remember: picture measurement + ⅛ inch − ½ inch. We are now cutting the final miter.

Cutting completed — The four sides are now ready for joining.

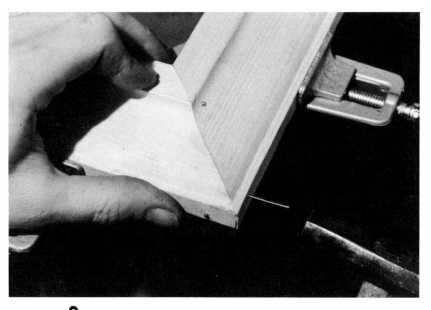

7 Gluing — Before clamping a long and a short side in the framing clamp we spread glue evenly on the miters.

8 Nailing — In this close-up you can see that the brads are driven in only up to the head to avoid scarring the frame. We use four 1¼ inch brads and place them as shown for maximum strength.

9 Setting — Using our nail set we drive the brad heads below the surface of the molding.

10 Nailing — We repeat the same joining operations on the opposite sides and are here joining the two halves; this final corner, when the brads have been set, completes our frame.

actual size

The completed frame

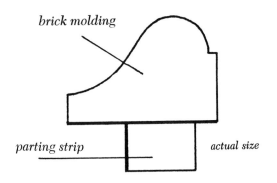

brick molding

parting strip   actual size

Brick

Brick molding makes an excellent frame when we combine it with a rabbet made of parting strip. Although it may be used with an insert as a frame for small oils, or in combination with other moldings for larger paintings, its simple profile works especially well with a mat as a frame for watercolors or drawings.

Build the parting strip rabbet first to the dimensions of your picture. The brick molding will overlap it to hold the picture. Since the parting strip will not show, there is no need to miter the corners; simple butt joints will do nicely.

Tools — Miter box, backsaw, hammer, yardstick, corner clamp.

Materials — One 8 foot piece brick molding, one 8 foot piece parting strip, glue, 1¼ and 1 inch brads.

1 Cutting — First we trim off one end of our stock. Note that the thin edge of our molding is next to the back of the miter box. The molding will be held firmly in this position for all our cuts.

2 Measuring — Along the thin, inside edge of our molding we measure the first long side. This measurement will be our picture measurement minus ½ inch to allow for overlap.

3 Cutting — We swing our saw and cut our second miter on the mark we have just measured.

4 **Measuring** — After trimming the end of our remaining stock we are here using the first side as a pattern to measure the second. Cutting a miter on this mark completes both long sides.

5 **Cutting** — We repeated steps 1 through 4 to make the two short sides; here the final miter is just about cut.

6 **Gluing and clamping** — We take one short side and one long side, spread glue evenly on the miters to be joined and place the pieces in the clamp. Tighten both sides of the clamp evenly and firmly and the corner is ready for nailing.

Cutting completed

7 **Nailing** — With the pieces tightly held in the clamp we drive one brad into each side. We drive the brads in only up to their heads to avoid scarring our frame.

63

8 Setting — We complete one half of our frame by setting the brad heads below the surface.

9 Joining — Repeating steps 6, 7 and 8 with the other two sides completes the second half. Here we are joining the two halves to complete the frame.

Ready to assemble

10 Nailing — With one brad driven part way into each side we check the position and then nail the rabbet permanently to the frame with a brad every 4 inches around the strip.

11 Gluing — We spread glue evenly on one face of the rabbet strip and center it on the back of our frame.

The completed frame

Variations

Strip frame no. 1

The strip, or band frame, is a comparatively new frame design which came into popular use about the time Mondrian was exhibiting his geometric compositions. Its clean lines complement the functional design of most contemporary paintings.

Here is a simple way to build a permanent strip frame for any pictures you have painted on panels of Masonite or wood. It consists of two wooden rectangles, one made of parting strip, which is fastened to the back of the panel, and one rectangle made of lattice strip, which goes around our panel and forms the frame proper.

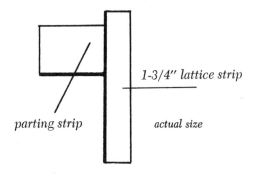

parting strip   *1-3/4″ lattice strip*

actual size

Tools — Miter box, backsaw, corner clamp, 4 C clamps, hammer.

Materials — One 8 foot piece 1¾ inch lattice strip, one 8 foot piece parting strip, glue, 1 inch brads.

Ready to frame – Our picture panel, the strips of stock and we are ready to begin.

1 Measuring — Using our panel as a pattern we measure the first long side of our parting strip.

2 Cutting — Because we are using simple butt joints on our backing strip, we are cutting both long sides at the same time to assure getting them exactly the same length.

3 Measuring — With the two sides we have already cut, held as shown, we again use the picture as a pattern to measure the short sides of our backing strip. Cut the sides and assemble the strip as shown on pages 17-18.

4 Positioning — After assembling our parting strip backing we position it on the back of our painting and draw a line around the inside edge. Then we begin cutting the frame proper.

5 Cutting — The lattice strip is held vertically in the miter box, and we trim the end, cutting our first 45° miter.

6 Measuring — The assembled backing strip becomes the pattern with which we are measuring the first long side of our frame.

7 Cutting — We have cut both long sides and repeated the same steps to make the short sides. Here we are cutting the final miter.

8 Joining — Joining these two halves and setting the brads completes the strip and we are ready to fasten the backing to our picture.

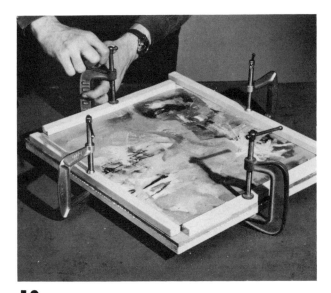

9 Gluing — Using the pencil line as a guide we coat the back of our panel evenly with glue. One side of the parting strip is also coated evenly with glue; both are allowed to dry and then given a second coat of glue over the same areas.

10 Clamping — While the second coat of glue is still wet we position the strip and clamp the two surfaces firmly with the C clamps. Be sure to use scrap pieces of parting strip to protect the painting and spread the clamp pressure evenly along the edge of the panel.

11 Assembly — After the parting strip and panel are dry — ours took about an hour — we fit our frame around it. With the picture face down on a level surface and working from the inside, we toenail 1 inch brads through the parting strip into the strip frame.

back view

The completed frame

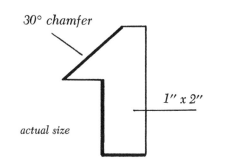

Strip frame no. 2

An ordinary 1 x 2 inch strip of wood can easily be made into a molding particularly suitable for band or strip frames. If you have a power saw, three simple cuts and you are ready to begin framing. If not, your lumber yard can convert the strip for you by following steps 1 and 2.

The main difference between this and an ordinary strip frame molding is a 30° chamfer which adds a bit of depth and enhances the proportions of the molding.

Tools — Miter box, backsaw, hammer, framing clamp.

Materials — One 8 foot piece 1 x 2 inch stock, glue, 1¼ inch brads.

30° chamfer

1" x 2"

actual size

1 Ripping — Setting our saw at the 30° mark, we adjust the guide so that we don't cut completely across the edge; the ⅛ inch left flat will provide an interesting accent to the angle created by the chamfer.

2 Ripping – Returning the saw blade to the 90° position we set it for a one inch deep cut. With the guide set ¼ inch from the blade, run the strip through. Then as you see in the photo the blade is set for a ¼ inch deep cut. With the guide ¼ inch from the blade, run the strip through to complete the rabbet.

3 Cutting — To begin making our frame we cut the first 45° miter near one end of our stock. Notice that the flat side of the molding is held firmly against the back of the miter box.

4 Measuring — From the inside of the miter we measure the first long side.

5 Cutting — We swing our saw to the opposite angle and make the cut which completes the first long side.

6 Measuring — After repeating step one to trim our remaining stock, we use the first side as a pattern to mark the second.

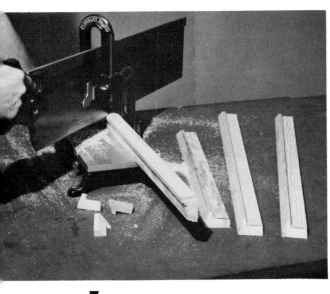

7 Cutting — Using the same measuring and cutting procedure that we used on the long sides, we are here making the final miter cut.

Cutting completed — What started as a simple 1 x 2 inch strip of lumber is now the four sides of our frame.

8 Gluing and clamping — After coating the mitered ends of one short and one long side of our frame, we tighten them firmly in the framing clamp ready for nailing.

9 Nailing — We drive two brads into each side of the corner making sure to leave the heads exposed; use your nail set to avoid scarring the frame.

10 Setting — With a nail set we drive the brad heads below the surface of the wood, completing the first half of our frame.

11 Joining — The remaining two sides of our frame are joined in the same manner as the first, and then the two halves are joined together to complete the frame.

Patinas

Texturing

Toning

Finishing

There are endless ways to finish picture frames. The possibilities are limited only by the ingenuity of the framer and the time at his disposal. All of the variations, however, are based generally on a two-step process. First the frame is textured, then it is toned to complement the picture.

One way to texture a frame is to cut into its surface. The cutting can range from a simple sanding to a complex carving. We can also use the frame as a base upon which to build a textured surface. The texture can extend from a simple thick coat of paint or gesso all the way to a complicated sculptured, rococo-type molding complete with roses and cupid's bows.

Beautiful modern finishes can be created using simple variations of both texturing methods either singly or in combination. On the following pages we demonstrate how you can prepare the surface of your frames, suitable for finishing in any number of ways.

Whether we carve our texture or build it up, the final finish of our frame will depend on color to present the picture at its best. Color or tone is usually applied to a frame in one or more coats of paint called *patinas*. The patina is basically gray but it may be tinted slightly with other colors. The color, however, should never be so strong as to overpower the picture. Neutrality is a good word to keep in mind when you mix any color for toning a frame. A good finish should harmonize with the picture; at the same time it should separate it from busy surroundings — but it must do all these things unobtrusively.

Before you actually start to work on your frame, read all the information on the following pages so that you get an idea of how all of this can be achieved. Then follow the step-by-step demonstration, mix a batch of basic patina and you are on your way in one of the most creative and exciting phases of picture framing.

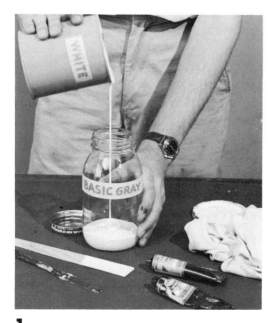

1 Base color — We start by pouring a quantity of the white into a large jar. The paint should be about the consistency of honey. You can thin it slightly with water if necessary.

2 Adding color — We add enough black to make a gray approximating the value of the gray tint below. This gray will be too cool, so we will add enough raw umber to get a more neutral tone. From this basic gray we will mix two patinas — one warm and one cool.

Note: — It is difficult to give exact quantities of color to use in mixing inasmuch as the tinting strength of tube color varies. However, one of the advantages of this type of finishing procedure is that should you get it too light or too dark, too warm or too cool, it can be easily adjusted with another coat of patina.

Mixing patinas

Heretofore the base of any patina was a thinned gesso. Anyone who has gone through the cookery necessary to make gesso can understand the joy some of the new paint products caused among people who frame pictures. For our patinas we use one of the vinyl-base household paints. It is readily available, water soluble and easy to mix, and brushes can be cleaned merely by rinsing them under the faucet. On the other hand, it dries quickly into a hard surface which is waterproof and lasting.

Any water soluble artists' colors such as casein, poster colors, etc., can be used to tint your patinas. The tinting colors we use are called Universal Colorants because they may be used to tint either oil or water base paint. Raw umber, ivory black, yellow ochre, ultramarine blue and iron oxide red are all you will need for most finishing jobs.

Materials — Our vinyl-base paint, raw umber and black colors, a jar, some rags, a mixing stick and we're ready to begin. For clarity in our photographs we are working on a painted table top; however, as we proceed you will see that a good supply of newspapers is normally a must.

Your basic gray when wet should match this tone.

Mixing warm and cool patinas

In most cases a frame is richer looking if its tone is built up with two or more patinas of varying color and temperature. The play of warm against cool, light against dark enhances the texture of the frame, and the vibrancy created avoids a flat "painted" look. Coffee cans and frozen food containers make excellent disposable mixing bowls. TV dinner trays divided in sections are especially handy for mixing small quantities of patina to finish a single frame or for making subtle adjustments in tone or color of a patina. The jars we use to store our patinas in are 8 ounce powder jars available in any drugstore.

Materials — Basic gray patina, two 8 ounce powder jars, yellow ochre, iron oxide red, ultramarine blue tinting colors, rags.

Warm patina

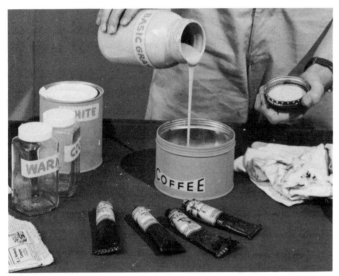

1 Base color — We pour a quantity of our basic patina into the mixing bowl.

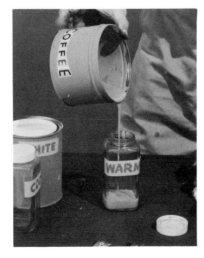

2 Adding color — To the basic patina we add a small amount of yellow ochre. The color is too intense so we add enough red to kill the yellowness. The final patina is a warm, brownish gray slightly darker in value than the basic gray.

3 Filling — We pour the patina into the jar labeled "Warm," and we are ready to mix the cool patina.

Cool patina

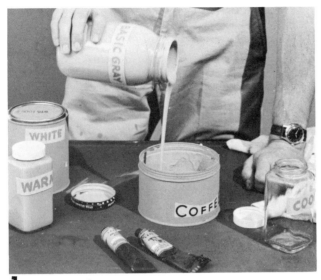

1 Base color — Following the same procedure, we first pour some basic gray into the mixing bowl.

2 Adding color — A small amount of ultramarine blue cools the patina enough. Use the blue sparingly; you may find it necessary to add a bit more raw umber to gray the patina to a more neutral color.

3 Filling — We pour the mixture into our jar.

Patinas — Here are our patinas, ready to use. If you intend to finish frames from time to time, mix up a good sized quantity of these three patinas. They provide a basic "palette" which has endless possibilities for varying the finishes of your frames to complement any picture.

Texturing — raking

Now that we have our patinas mixed and ready to use, we are ready to take the first step in finishing an actual frame. For this demonstration we are using the drip cap frame we showed you how to build on pages 24 through 29. This particular frame offers us the chance to show you three ways of texturing, plus the use of the patinas and powdered gold. Keep in mind as you work, however, that these procedures will work with any frame. Read over the methods we use and then follow the steps. It won't be long before you are finding your own variations and creating exciting finishes for the frames you build.

Tools — Paint scraper, palette knife, wood rasp, triangular file, paintbrush.

Materials — Wood filler, sandpaper, walnut oil stain.

Tools — We call the first texturing method we show you "raking" because we actually rake the surface of our frame. You can use any sharp, pointed instrument to cut the texture into the wood; however, we recommend the paint scraper as the easiest and most effective.

Filing — To convert the paint scraper into a texturing rake we file a series of V-shaped teeth into the edge with our triangular file. Keep the teeth uneven; too much regularity will make the texture monotonous.

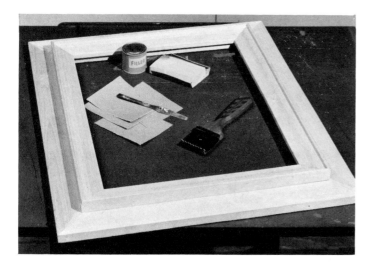

Ready for raking — For this finish we are going to rake the surface of the 1 x 4. Our frame, sandpaper, wood filler, the converted paint scraper and we are ready to go to work.

76

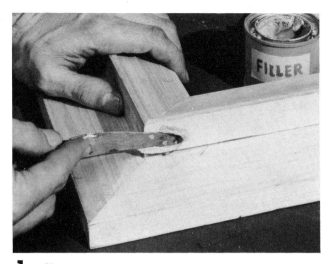

1 Filling — We start by filling the nail holes with wood dough which we force into the holes with a palette knife. Press hard to make sure the holes are solidly filled. If there are any small gaps in the mitered corners, fill them also.

2 Sanding — Excess wood dough can be sanded off when dry — about 10 or 15 minutes.

3 Raking — We use the paint scraper to rake the surface of the 1 x 4, making a series of valleys. Rake *with the grain* from the miters toward the center with short, firm strokes — the more grooves the better. Try to keep the texture from becoming too uniform.

Close-up — In this close-up you can see how the teeth of the rake dig into the wood. Notice that the texture is not mechanical or regular.

4 Sanding — After raking the entire 1 x 4 we sand the surface lightly to remove the heaviest burrs. This is not a finished sanding and should not be too smooth.

Ready for staining — With the surface raked and sanded we are ready to stain the 1 x 4.

5 Staining — We now brush in the oil stain. Cover only the surface and edges of the 1 x 4. Later on we will show you another way to texture the drip cap.

Close-up — Notice how the stain soaks into the wood. It will provide a permanent dark value which we will use to control the final tone of our frame. Drying time varies, so follow the manufacturer's recommendations. It is important that the frame be *thoroughly dry* before proceeding.

6 Rasping — The second texturing method requires only our wood rasp. We are using it to score lightly the raised outside edge of the drip cap. The rasp is held flat and pushed diagonally across the surface creating a series of ridges. Caution: Work lightly; too much pressure will break down the edge of your frame.

7 Sanding — A light sanding completes the textures we are going to cut into the surface of our frame. We are now ready to show you how to build up a texture on the sloping surface of the drip cap.

Texturing — gesso

The basis of this method of texturing a frame is very simple: a coat of paint, into which the texture is scored, scratched or modeled.

Building up a texture used to mean many coats of gesso or thick casein paint. The first is an involved, time consuming process, and the second, while quicker, has the annoying property of chipping or flaking off.

Looking for a way to build up textures, with all the good points of gesso and none of its complexities, we found that the same vinyl paint we used to mix our patinas worked perfectly when we used it in its undiluted form.

Materials — For this demonstration, our vinyl paint, a nylon brush and a pocket comb are all we need.

Other texturing tools — Look around your home; almost anything that can make a mark will serve as a texturing tool. Experiment with everything from your fingers to a piece of window screening.

1 Applying gesso — We brush on a thick coat of our vinyl paint "gesso." This must dry 10 to 20 minutes or until the paint will retain a scratch without filling in.

2 Painting insert — While the gesso is drying we give the insert a coat of the white vinyl. You may find a little water is needed to thin the paint to an easy brushing consistency.

3 Combing gesso — We break our comb in half to make it easier to handle and, working from the outside edge, draw it quickly across the partially dried paint. Continue combing until the whole surface of the drip cap is textured to your satisfaction.

Textures — Here are two textures easily created with a comb. The first is made by scoring the paint once with the coarse teeth of the comb while the second is made with several passes of the comb over the surface.

How much texture you should make depends on your own taste and the requirements of the picture you are framing. Remember that the frame *must not compete* with the picture for your viewers' interest.

Toning

Our frame is textured, the gesso is dry and we are now ready to use the warm and cool patinas in the final stage of finishing.

1 First patina — We use the cool patina first because we want to finish with a warm tone to go with the warm quality of the picture we are framing. If our picture were cool in tone we would use the warm patina first. Thin the patina slightly with water and brush well into the valleys.

2 Sanding — After the patina is dry — in about 25 or 30 minutes — we sand the whole frame with medium sandpaper — enough to show some of the dark understain on the ridges but not enough to dig the patina out of the valleys.

3 Second patina — With our warm patina we now cover a small section of the frame. Before this dries we wipe it lightly with a rag, exposing the first patina and some of the understain. We repeat this process around the whole frame as many times as is necessary to arrive at the tone we want.

4 Sanding — The last sanding controls the final tone; the more patina you take off the darker the value of the finish.

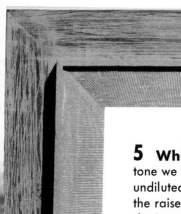

Note: — Now is a good time to try the frame on our picture. If the frame is too dark because we have sanded too much, we repeat steps 3 and 4 and sand again. With successive coats of light or dark, warm or cool, you can achieve any color or value to harmonize with any picture.

5 Whiting edge — Since our frame is the right tone we now dress it up by dipping a small pad in the undiluted white vinyl paint and wipe it quickly along the raised edge of the drip cap. Drag the pad lightly; don't try to fill the grooves solidly.

6 Mixing gold — We have poured a small amount of bronzing liquid into a pan — a frozen food container serves well — and we add enough Venus powdered gold to make a mixture of good brushing consistency.

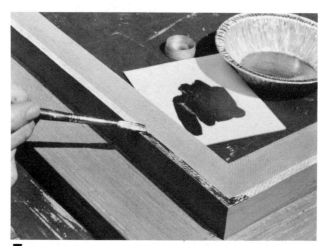

7 Applying gold — We work some of the gold out of our brush onto a scrap piece of cardboard or newspaper before applying it to the frame. Working quickly, we "dry-brush" the edge, just hitting the high spots. This touch of gold, if not overdone, will give our frame richness. Later on we show you how to use gold leaf and wax gilt, two additional ways for you to add luster to your frames.

8 Waxing — Over the thoroughly dry, finished frame we rub a coat of paste wax. The wax is to protect, not polish, the finish, and its satinlike sheen serves to pull the tone together into a mellow antique patina.

The finished frame

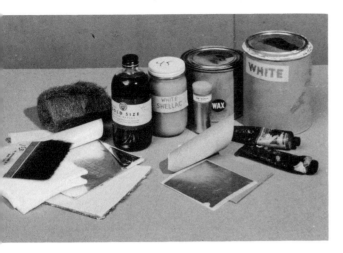

Materials — In addition to the gold leaf itself we need gold size, white shellac, our warm patina, vinyl white, colorants, steel wool, absorbent cotton, Venus bronzing powder and wax.

1 First patina— We first give the entire frame a coat of warm patina. Note that the clamshell flat has already been raked and stained. We are going to leaf the inner face of the insert.

Gilding

As with anything in framing, there are many ways to give your frames a touch of gold. On page 82 we showed you one way; here are three more methods of gilding you can try. Each has its own characteristics. Experiment with all three to find out what they are like and how you can use them in finishing your frames. Gilding is fun and it won't be long before you are finding your own creative uses for this fascinating phase of picture framing.

Two of the gilding methods use metal leaf. In the first demonstration we use gold leaf on a paper backing, specially prepared for gilding in the wind. This leaf is pure 23 carat gold and is a little more expensive than the synthetic leaf; however, we recommend it because of its ease in handling.

The second gold leaf we show you is a little harder to handle, but with practice it can be mastered. As you gain confidence you will probably use this less expensive synthetic leaf for most of your frame gilding.

For a quick gilding job try the wax gilding method. You will be well pleased with the richness of this simple process.

2 Steel wooling — After the patina dries we lightly steel wool the surface to be gilded.

3 Second patina — To our warm patina we add enough white to lighten it and coat the insert again.

4 Steel wooling — A second steel wooling leaves the surface smooth enough for a good gilding. Repeat the patinizing and steel wooling as many times as is necessary to provide a smooth surface.

5 Mixing shellac — Metal leaf always looks better when it is applied over a colored ground. Usually red works best under gold, while silver leaf looks best over a black or ochre ground. We are here adding our red colorant to the white shellac which will dry quickly and evenly.

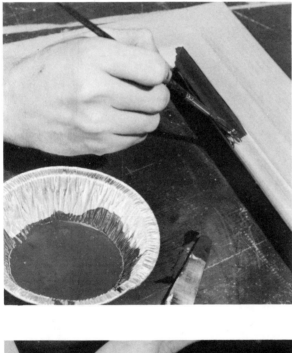

6 Applying shellac — The area to be gilded is being given a coat of the red-colored shellac. Work quickly to avoid streaks or pile-ups.

7 Applying gold size — Here in the final stage of preparation we are coating the entire red area with transparent gold size. The frame is then set aside to dry for about 1 to 2 hours.

8 Testing size — It is extremely important that the size be in the right condition before applying the leaf. Size which is too wet will dissolve the leaf, while a too dry size will result in a weak gild, prone to rubbing off. Test the size after about an hour by touching your knuckle to it. When it is just slightly tacky it is ready. Gilders refer to it as "whistling" tacky.

9 Applying leaf — Holding our paper-backed leaf as shown, we gently roll it against the sized area.

10 Pressing backing — We press the backing, very lightly, to make sure the leaf is completely covering the sized surface.

11 Removing backing — The gold leaf will adhere to the size while we gently peel off the paper backing. Repeat these steps around the entire frame, overlapping each application slightly.

12 Patching — As you gild, save the paper backing. The small bits of excess leaf can be used to patch any skips or misses. The ragged appearance causes no worry — the extra leaf will come off easily when we burnish the gilded area with our absorbent cotton. It will adhere only to the surface covered with size.

13 – 15 Alternate method — These photos show one more advantage to using paper-backed leaf. We have cut the leaf into easy-to-handle strips with a razor blade. Cut the strips slightly wider than the surface to be gilded, then follow the same steps to apply.

13

14

15

16 Leaf applied — The insert has been gilded and is ready to be burnished to clean up the ragged appearance.

17 Burnishing — We burnish the gild with absorbent cotton. Rub lightly; this step is to clean up the edges and lightly buff the gold.

The completed gild

- -

Synthetic leaf

1 Gilder's Tip — A Gilder's Tip is a flat, wide, soft bristled brush used to transfer the leaf from its backing to the frame. The Tip holds the leaf with a charge of static electricity which is created by brushing the Tip lightly across your hair before touching it to the leaf. The surface of our frame has been prepared following steps 1 through 8, and we are here applying the synthetic gold leaf. The book of leaf is held as shown and the leaf scored through with the fingernail. After passing the brush lightly over the hair, the cut strip will stick to it and can be shifted to the surface of the frame. This is a tricky operation and will take some practice. Try to work in a room free from drafts or the leaf will act like the will-o'-the-wisp.

2 Sanding — We have gilded and burnished the frame and for this finish are sanding the leaf lightly. Note the effect created when some of the red ground is allowed to show through the gold. This is one variation; there are others. A light spatter of black also works well. Experimentation will show you more.

Wax gilding

Ordinarily gilding is an operation most beginning framers avoid because of its complexities and the skill needed to apply a good gild. The methods we have shown you thus far have, we hope, dispelled some of the mystery and awe surrounding this phase of framing. If you still feel somewhat timid about using metal leaf, here is the simplest way to add gilding to your framing repertoire. Now even this simple method can be complicated with cookery, special waxes and varnishes, but we have found this easy-to-follow procedure perfectly satisfactory and lasting. All you need is a good grade of paste wax, some bronzing powder, a TV dinner tray and some rags.

1 Applying patina — We start by preparing our frame with a coat of patina.

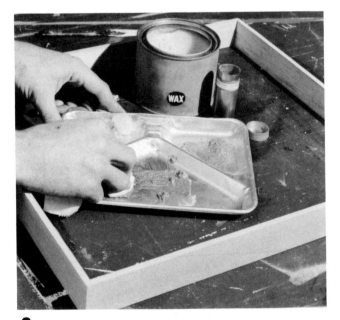

2 Mixing — Our gild is mixed by rubbing the wax into some of the bronzing powder which we have poured into the mixing tray.

3 Applying gilt — Simply rubbing the wax gilt mixture over our thoroughly dry frame completes this gild.

4 Buffing — The wax gilt is allowed to dry. We then buff the frame with a clean, soft rag to bring out its rich, mellow sheen.

The finished frame

Mounting prints

Prints, drawings, photographs, maps and other things you may want to keep are often printed on paper which doesn't have sufficient body to bear up under the usage of time. They can be made more substantial and permanent by mounting them on a rigid support.

The mounting procedure we show you here is the best all-around method we have found. It works well for anything from a photograph to a canvas, and you can mount your picture on almost any surface. Because we will eventually frame our demonstration print in a small frame, we chose Upsom board as a firm but lightweight backing. Where weight is not a consideration, Masonite or plywood makes exceptionally good supports. Old canvases of either sentimental or actual value can also be preserved and protected by mounting them in this way, and with a little care even small tears can be almost completely hidden.

For the adhesive we recommend one of two types: one is a synthetic latex, the other has a casein base. Both are used in the same way and are clean and easy to handle. They are water soluble, making clean-up of brushes and working areas quick and simple. They store well and, most important, have wonderful holding power.

Mounting prints is not difficult if you will observe two simple rules: first, have plenty of newspapers handy; second, *keep your hands and tools clean.*

1 Measuring — Measure your print carefully and check it for squareness, then with your yardstick mark off its size on your Upsom board; or as we have done, since our print was square, simply lay your print on the board and trace around it.

2 Cutting — We hold the mat knife vertically against the straight edge and cut the Upsom board to size.

3 Gluing — We quickly brush glue on one side of our Upsom board. When the surface has been covered . . .

4 Gluing — . . . we even out the glue by brushing it over lightly in one direction. The trick in gluing is not to get too much or too little glue on the surface so that it will hold well but not squeeze out when rolled.

5 Positioning — If your print is very large wet it first to avoid bubbles, then quickly place the print on the glued surface. Here care must be taken to get your print in the right position — because once down it can be moved very little.

6 Rolling — Starting in the middle, with firm pressure, we work toward the outer edges, rolling out bubbles and excess glue — with practice there won't be much. Be sure not to get glue on the roller — you can cover your print with a light sheet of paper to prevent this.

7 Pressing — If you mount only an occasional print it is possible to use a clean, soft rag in place of the roller. However, greater care must be taken not to damage the surface.

8 Clamping — We place a clean sheet of paper over our print and clamp it between two pieces of ¾ inch plywood for an hour. (One board and a stack of books for a weight would work as well.) If any bubbles occur, smooth them out with your finger and place under pressure again.

Cutting mats

Watercolors and drawings to be shown at their best require a mat. Matboard is available at any art supply store and comes in a variety of colors. It usually has a pebble finish and each side is a different color. The most useful color combination is white on one side and gray on the other. Watercolors are generally matted with white, but in many cases a cream or gray mat will heighten the color or the over-all effect. The matboard you buy is usually about ⅛ inch thick and can be used as soon as it is cut. For the times you may want a thicker mat, your lumber yard can supply you with Upson board or Homosote. These all make very handsome mats when the inside edge is beveled and they are given a coat of vinyl or rubber-base paint of appropriate color.

A mat should be wide enough to separate the picture from busy surroundings without being so wide that it makes the picture appear smaller. While requirements may vary for each picture, we have found a 3 x 4 inch or 2½ x 3 inch mat will work well with most paintings. Generally a mat is the same width at the top and sides and slightly wider at the bottom, thus a 3 x 4 inch mat is 3 inches wide at the top and sides and 4 inches wide at the bottom.

Practice cutting small mats out of scraps of board, then follow the procedure we show you, and you will soon be cutting professional looking mats.

Materials — The mat we are going to cut is made from a piece of Upsom board which we have given a coat of our warm patina. A straightedge, yardstick, mat knife, pencil, compass, our picture and we are ready to begin.

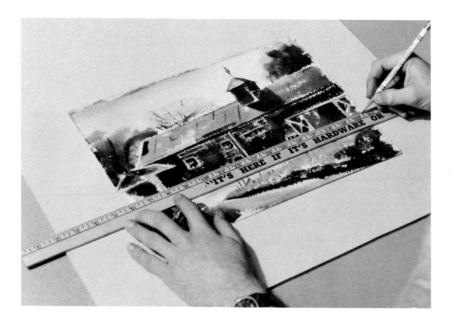

1 Measuring — We are going to make a 3 x 4 inch mat so we are here adding 6 inches to the width of our painting. Place the 6 inch mark of the yardstick on the left edge of the picture; the over-all width of your mat is at the right edge. For the height we add 7 inches.

2 Measuring — With our matboard face down on the flat, clean surface of our table we mark the over-all dimensions. Do all of your measuring and marking on the back of your board to keep the face clean.

3 Cutting — We hold our straightedge firmly on the marks we have measured and with the mat knife held at a right angle to the matboard we draw it along the edge.

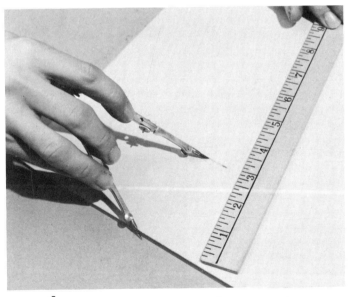

4 Setting compass — After setting the compass at 3 inches we hold the metal point against the edge of the mat and draw the compass along the top and sides.

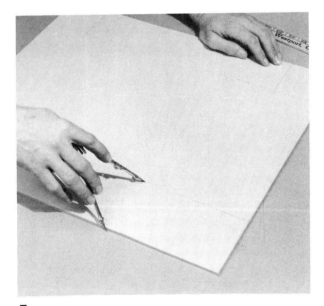

5 Ruling — The bottom line is drawn in the same way when we have reset the compass to 4 inches. Notice that all the lines are carried out to the edges to allow us to check our dimensions before we begin cutting.

6 **Sharpening knife** – To avoid a ragged edge next to our picture it is important to cut the inside edges in one stroke. We find a whetstone invaluable for sharpening our blade between each cut.

7 **Cutting** – Two nails hold our straightedge steady for our cut. We push the point of our knife, at an angle, into the matboard about ⅛ inch beyond the corner. This overcutting insures sharp corners, and because this mat is beveled, the overcut will only be about 1/16 of an inch on the face of the mat and will not be noticeable.

8 **Cutting** – Holding the knife firmly at a constant angle we make the cut in one smooth stroke. When we get to the end of the line we cut ⅛ inch beyond the corner. The remaining three sides are cut in the same way. Remember to make all these inside cuts in one stroke to avoid a ragged edge. If you do make a slightly rough cut it can be smoothed with a light sanding.

9 Taping — To help us position our picture in the mat we attach a piece of masking tape along the under edge so that half of it extends beyond the edge of the paper. We do this at the top and bottom edges.

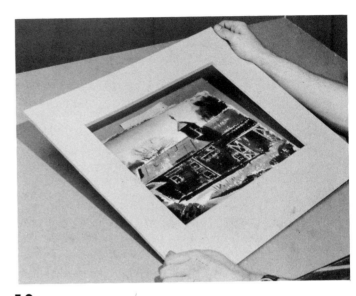

10 Positioning mat — We now place the mat in the right position over the picture and press it firmly against the strips of masking tape. These strips allow us to turn both mat and picture over for a final check.

11 Taping — After checking the position of the picture we tape the four sides with additional strips of tape. We have used masking tape for this final taping; however, a more permanent mounting can be made using gummed brown paper tape. Simply moisten the strips of tape and glue the strips down. The masking tape strips used in step 9 are removed when they have served their purpose.

The finished picture — Our finished picture, matted and ready to be framed.

Covering mats and inserts

Inserts and mats are really frames within frames — as such they may be finished using any of the methods we have shown you for finishing the frames themselves. With imaginative treatment of the insert, picture and frame can be made even more impressive. Experiment with a variety of finishes; remember, however, that because they are next to the picture, restraint is needed to make sure the insert or mat complements the frame without overpowering the picture.

In this respect a fabric covering is very often the perfect solution. Raw linen, monkscloth and sometimes burlap are often used because of their neutral tonality, but for certain pictures other fabrics may be used to achieve very fine effects.

There are two generally accepted ways to cover inserts. In the first, the strips of molding are covered with fabric before joining. This results in neat miters, but the cloth on the molding stands a good chance of being damaged or soiled during assembly. In the second method, which we prefer, the insert is completely assembled before being covered. This avoids excess handling of the molding, and with a little practice the corners can be mitered perfectly with your mat knife or razor blade.

A mat may be covered in the same way; however, because of its width, it usually looks better when it is covered using a single piece of fabric without mitering the corners. On the next several pages we show you the methods we have found best for covering both mats and inserts.

Tools — Scissors, mat knife, brush.

Materials — Raw linen, glue.

1 Cutting — We start by cutting four strips of linen. The strips should be about 2 inches longer than the sides to be covered and wide enough to cover both the face and the entire rabbet.

2 Gluing — Working carefully from miter to miter we brush an even coat of glue over the face of one side of the insert. The strip of linen is then laid in the position shown. Notice that it overlaps the corners and edges. The four sides are covered in the same manner. Press the cloth into the glue *lightly*. Too much pressure will cause the glue to come through the cloth and make an unsightly blemish which cannot be cleaned up.

3 Cutting — With our knife sharpened, we start in the inside corner of each miter and cut through *both* thicknesses of cloth where they overlap. Cutting through both pieces at once ensures a perfect match.

4 Finishing miter — Lifting the top piece of linen we remove the excess bottom piece and press the top piece back into position in the partially dried glue. Repeat these steps in each corner.

5 Trimming rabbet — After mitering all four corners we spread glue along the entire rabbet and fold the fabric around the inside edge. The excess cloth is then trimmed off with our knife.

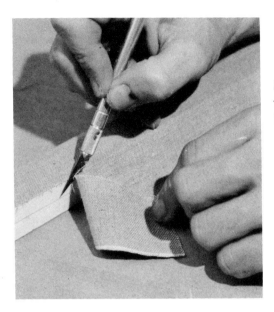

6 Trimming edge— The frame will hold the insert, so there is no need to cover the outside edge. Here the excess linen is being trimmed flush with the top of our insert.

The covered insert

- -

Covering mats

Materials - The materials and tools needed to cover mats are exactly the same as we used to cover the insert in the previous demonstration.

1 Cutting — We spread our linen out on the flat, clean surface of our table and cut a piece about 1 inch larger than our mat all around.

2 Gluing — With the linen cut we coat the front of our mat with a thin, even coat of glue.

3 Positioning mat — The linen is again spread flat and the mat placed glue side down, centered and pressed *lightly* in place.

4 Smoothing — Turning the mat and linen face up we go over the entire face smoothing the linen in place. We work quickly and very *lightly* to avoid unsightly glue spots. Here again too much pressure will cause the glue to seep through the cloth.

5 Cutting — To facilitate gluing the outside edge a small piece of material is cut from each outside corner. The cut is made at a 45° angle to the corner so that there is no overlapping when the cloth is folded over the edge.

6 Gluing — Here you see the back of the mat being given a coat of glue. Notice the angle of the cut we made in the previous step. Coat the entire outside edge with glue.

7 Smoothing — We now fold the outside edges of our material over the back of the mat and press them *firmly* in place.

8 Cutting — With our mat still face down and the outside edges glued we cut out the "window." We leave about 1 inch extra to fold over the back of the mat.

9 Cutting — Starting about 1/8 inch in from the corner to allow for the thickness of our matboard, we make a single miter cut to the inside edge of the material.

10 Gluing — Now we coat the entire inside edge of the mat with glue.

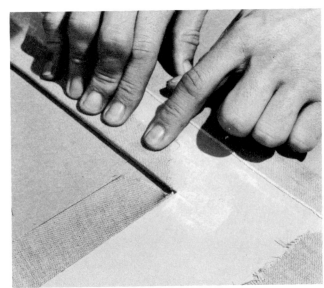

11 Smoothing — The inside material is folded over and we are pulling it tightly against the edge of the mat. The ⅛ inch we allowed in step 9 will pull tight against the corner resulting in a slightly rounded, neat frame for our picture. If we had cut right up to the corner, a gap would appear at this stage which would detract from the quality of our mat.

The covered mat

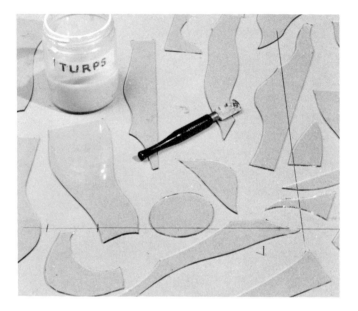

Glass cutting

There is something about cutting glass that frightens most of us. However, if you will get a piece of glass to practice on and follow these four basic rules you will be an expert in fifteen minutes.

1. Always work on a *perfectly flat surface*. A piece of carpet or a thick bed of newspapers will level most table tops.
2. Clean your glass. If it is new it will probably be clean, but if you are using old glass be sure to wash it.
3. Always dip your cutter in turpentine or kerosene before each stroke. This aids the cutting wheel to make a clean cut.
4. Never go over a cut. Make it right the first time.

Now relax and cut some freehand shapes in your practice piece like the ones in our illustration. Then try some cuts against your straightedge. Nothing we can say will teach you as much as this practice, so be sure to do it before following the demonstration.

Tools – Materials— Straightedge, yardstick, pencil, glass cutter, glass, turpentine, rag.

1 **Layout** — We have leveled our table top and have drawn a right angle on it. Along one side we mark the two dimensions of our picture, in this case 8 and 11 inches.

2 **Nailing** — Since it is difficult to hold a straightedge firmly on glass, we position ours for the cut and drive in one brad at either end to hold it steady.

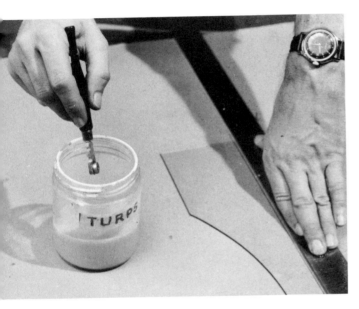

3 **Dipping** — We bring one end of our glass up to the 11 inch mark and under the straightedge. Just before making the cut we dip our cutter in turps.

4 **Cutting** — Holding the straightedge against the brads and the cutter vertically against the straightedge, we draw the cutter with firm pressure across the glass. Your pressure is right when a clear "scratch" sound is heard.

5 Tapping — With the cutter we give a sharp rap on the under side of the glass below the cut. This starts the break.

6 Positioning — We place the spot where the break has started over a pencil, with a little pressure applied to either side . . .

7 Breaking — . . . snap! Our cut has been cleanly made and the glass parts down the full length. We move our glass under the straight-edge to the 8 inch mark and make the second cut the same way.

Materials — The raw materials from one attic.

Antique frames

Attics, cellars, secondhand stores and junk shops are wonderful hunting grounds for old frames. These old frames are seldom usable as they are found, and restoring (that is, returning the frame to its original condition) is a complex operation. Even then, the ornateness of most of the carving is usually too much for any painting to overcome. However, they are generally well constructed and the basic design of their moldings, with a little modification, can be made suitable for even the most contemporary paintings.

Our purpose here is to show you how to use these "junk" frames as a starting point from which you can create distinctive, one of a kind, frames combining the richness of the past with the tastes of today.

The main thing to keep in mind when you are finishing old frames is that there are no rules or set procedures. Each frame will be a different problem with its own solutions dictated by the design of the frame and the picture you are framing. The trick is to take advantage of the unique good features of your frame while getting rid of the distracting overdecoration so typical of Victorian picture frames.

1 Disassembling — Sometimes when finishing an old frame it is necessary to rebuild it. Here the insert has been knocked down and we are taking the frame itself apart.

2 Reassembling — After cleaning the old dried glue from the miters, we reconstruct the frame. Note the framing clamps used at each corner to ensure squareness and maximum strength.

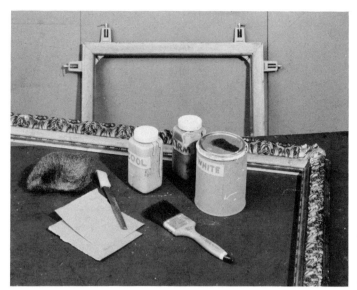

Ready to begin — Our patinas, white vinyl gesso, brush, steel wool, sandpaper and a wood rasp are the tools and materials we need to complete the job. As a safety measure, we have wrapped the handle of the rasp with tape.

3 Rasping — It takes determination seemingly to destroy the "beautiful" carving, but the first step is to rasp the entire surface of the frame. Work vigorously until all of the decoration has been taken down and softened.

4 Applying gesso — Here we are giving the rasped frame a coat of thick, undiluted vinyl paint. Work the paint well into the valleys; as you can see, this step is a further softening of the carving. We are now getting somewhere — the carving is now a texture rather than flowers and bows.

5 Wiping edge — The inner edge of this molding has a good simple curve, so before the vinyl is completely dry we wipe it off partially to allow some of the gold leaf to show through.

6 Toning — After the vinyl gesso has dried thoroughly we tone the frame with successive wipes of our warm and cool patina. From this point on, the frame is finished as we did the demonstration on pages 81 and 82.

7 Sanding — Our frame is finished, so we begin by sanding the insert. We found a layer of silver leaf under the gold which we will take advantage of by sanding only enough to expose parts of the silver and keeping parts of the gold. Note how the two colors create an interesting texture.

8 Toning insert — A coat of patina is now given the entire sanded surface of the insert.

9 Steel wooling — When the patina has dried we go over the surface lightly with our steel wool. This patina, gold and silver finish will go nicely with the frame and picture. This is a good example of taking what you may find on the frame and modifying it only enough to make it work well.

The finished frame

Antique frame no. 2

To show you another type of frame and finish we have rebuilt a small frame and insert. For this finish we need our patinas, brush, bronzing powder, wax, sandpaper and a rag.

1 Sanding — Under the rather frightening black enamel we find an excellently applied gesso ground. We sand the entire insert enough to get rid of the black and soften the "cute" carving.

2 Wax gilding — The white gesso we have uncovered provides an excellent ground for a wax gild. This simple step completes the insert. Now to see what can be done for the frame itself.

3 Applying patina — We raked the frame to incorporate the nicks and scars into a texture, gave it a coat of cool patina and are now dry-brushing the surface with a lighter value warm patina. This in turn will be lightly sanded and waxed to give us the effect you see in the completed frame.

The completed frame

Hanging your pictures

Assembling and wiring are the final steps to getting our pictures where we want them — on the wall. The job is a simple one but of great importance in presenting your pictures at their best. A good job of assembly will actually help strengthen and reinforce your frames, while a poorly fitted picture will not stand the ravages of dust and time for long.

Cleanliness, careful workmanship and these easy-to-follow steps will result in framed pictures whose fine appearance will last many years.

Materials — In addition to our picture, glass and frame we will need a yardstick, pliers, scissors, ice pick, X-acto knife or razor blade, rags, wrapping paper, screw eyes, picture wire, 1 inch brads and a piece of matboard backing the same size as our matted picture.

1 Backing picture — We have cleaned our glass thoroughly, placed it and our picture into the frame and are here installing the backing board. Note: Be sure the rabbet is free of any unevenness. When glass is used, a small drop of excess glue or paint will prevent even contact and eventually cause the glass to crack.

2 Nailing — We use our pliers to push the brads through the backing board into the frame. This method of inserting brads avoids hammering the frame and should be used whenever possible. Note the masking tape wrapped around the pliers to protect the frame. Place the brads as flat as possible with just enough angle to go through the backing board. After placing one brad in each side turn the picture and check its position; if it's all right, place brads about 3 inches apart all around the frame.

3 Wetting paper—We have cut the brown wrapping paper about an inch larger than our frame and are here wetting it with a rag and water. This slight dampening will cause the paper to stretch so that when it dries on the frame it will shrink to a smooth, neat, dustproof cover.

4 Gluing — We now spread an even coat of glue around the back edge of our frame.

5 Positioning paper — During the gluing step our paper has stretched, so we now place it in position and smooth it out. It is not necessary to get the paper drum tight — remember, it will tighten up as it dries.

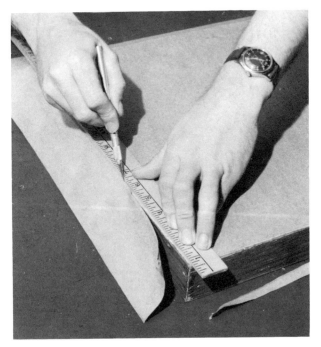

6 Trimming—Using our yardstick as a straightedge, we are trimming off the excess paper. You can see how well the paper tightened up when it dried.

7 Measuring — To locate our screw eyes, we place a mark about one-third down from the top of our frame.

8 Punching — To make it easier to start our screw eyes we use our ice pick as an awl to punch a hole at each mark.

9 Installing eyes — A brad placed through the screw eye makes it easier to turn it in as far as it will go.

10 Wiring — Our picture wire is cut about 8 inches longer than the frame and is looped *twice* through each screw eye. The double looping strengthens the wire at the point of most strain.

11 Wiring — We then twist the remaining wire back on itself about 3 inches.

12 Ready to hang — The little bit of slack left in the wire helps the picture center itself on the hanger. Too much slack, however, will show above the frame and should be avoided, while a too tight wire will cause the picture to slide on the hanger and obstinately refuse to hang straight.

- -

Wiring a large picture — In wiring a large, heavy picture it is advisable to support it from four points as shown here. The wire is fastened to the two bottom screw eyes and allowed to pass freely through the eyes in the sides. When the picture hangs, the pressure exerted actually helps pull the frame together. The wire running through the center is to prevent the top and bottom from springing apart during handling. You may find it better to hang large pictures from two hooks to help carry the weight and assure a level picture.

Examples

On this and the following pages are shown a variety of picture frames. Not all of them are taken from the demonstrations in this book, but all are based on the principles we have discussed.

We present these examples to show you that it is not always mandatory to "follow the rules"; rather it is more important to let each picture dictate its own needs. Notice particularly the variety of textures, materials and molding silhouettes and how each frame carries out the feeling expressed in the painting it surrounds.

The key word is still neutrality. A frame should complement the painting without being gaudy or show-offish.

This portrait by Ben Stahl calls for a frame which echoes the geometric treatment in the painting. Our first drip cap frame, which we also used for the finishing demonstrations, works excellently when we add a natural linen insert. The insert provides a good transition between the texture of the painting and the frame and also softens the whole effect and prevents its becoming too severe.

Ben Stahl — Portrait — Collection of Mr. and Mrs. Ed Reinhardt

Charles Reid — Life Class — Collection of the artist

A coat of gray patina and a raw umber glaze are all that is needed to give the textures on this handsome antique frame a wonderfully mellowed character. Notice how the delicate detailing of the frame beautifully complements the strong, direct and spontaneous feeling of the picture.

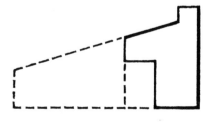

A single strip of drip cap ripped in half provides enough molding for this frame and the one on page 119. The lower half of the molding, rabbeted as shown, sets off this black and white reproduction of a Dong Kingman water-color. The linen covered mat is surrounded by a frame which is finished in flat black and has a wax gild on the sloping face. Notice how the linear quality of the frame handsomely complements the strong pattern and design in the picture.

Erno Czako — Landscape — Collection of Mr. and Mrs. Hal Rogers

To keep this very active painting contained, the thin top edge of the molding has been treated with pure white. The 1 x 4 backing has been raked and patinized to provide a harmonious transition from the wall to the picture. The whole effect is further enhanced by the frame's reverse design which is in keeping with the tapestry-like character of the painting.

Ed Reinhardt — Crucible — Collection of Mr. and Mrs. Albert Dorne

The powerful design of this abstract painting is beautifully enhanced by this striking frame. The wider inner edge of the molding is wax gilded with a cool coin gold while the thin outer edge has been gold leafed and sanded. This is the finish we demonstrated on page 87. The gold tones complement the rich reds in the picture and a soft velvety separation between the two temperatures of gold is created by painting the deep channel black.

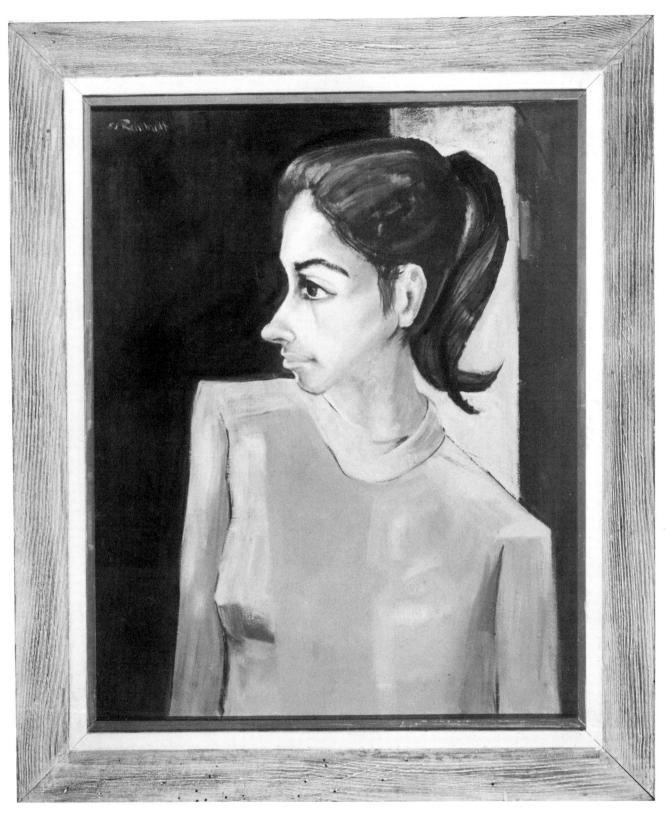

Ed Reinhardt — Elsie — Collection of Miss Elsie Lengyel

Here is a portrait which is quite different in feeling from the soft, muted study on page 115. The strong structural design of the figure and its environment requires a frame with a distinctly linear character.

The finish is an easy one to achieve. The entire frame is coated with a light, warm patina; then the raked surface of the 1 x 4 is wiped with a darker tone to create the contrast which emphasizes the angular quality in both the frame and the composition. A thin, soft gold insert brings out the best in the warm reds and browns and adds richness.

Ed Reinhardt — Spring Haze — Collection of Mr. and Mrs. Hal Rogers

Even though this picture is full of movement, a simple strip frame is all that is needed to present it at its best. Any more ornamentation would compete with the activity within the painting and rob it of some of its vigor.

The frame is simply finished with a wax gild and the depth of the 1¾ inch lattice strip gives the picture a pleasant feeling of volume when it is hanging on the wall.

Alfred Chadbourn — Lobster Buoys — Collection of the artist

This painting, having an extremely strong pattern, would look well in almost any frame which echoed its angular character. Notice, however, that although strong and geometric in character, the molding does not compete with the picture because it is finished with a simple light-over-dark patina and a minimum of texture.

E. Michael Mitchell — Study — Collection of Mrs. E. P. Reinhardt

To accentuate the delicacy of tone and line in this study we found the antique frame we used in the demonstration on pages 108 and 109 a good solution. In combination with a gray mat the flat bands of the frame have a linear quality which is in keeping with the character of a drawing, at the same time the classic symmetry of the design emphasizes the spontaneity of the medium.

Franklin R. Jones — November — Collection of the artist

For this picture which is handled in a traditional manner, an antique frame is just the thing. The familiarity of the scene and the directness of the technique have a warmth which the mellowness of the frame complements.

William C. Logan — Bois de Boulogne — Collection of the artist

The handling in this delightful picture creates a textural surface which the grain of the barn wood frame makes even more light and airy. The flat decorative quality is further enhanced by the frame's reverse design. In this case the silvery sheen of the weathered wood was a perfect foil for the cool blues and greens in the painting so that we used it "as is" with no further treatment. The raised molding was toned with a coat of off-white vinyl paint.

Sources of materials

Because most of the items used in our method of making and finishing your own picture frames are easily obtained, it is no longer necessary to buy and store large quantities of materials.

Most of the materials can be found in your local art supply store, hardware, paint shop or lumber yard. You will also find many of these items listed in the larger mail order catalogues and the classified section of your telephone directory.

Should you have any difficulty locating a particular item, your local merchant can often suggest an excellent substitute; if not the following list of sources will be helpful.

Adhesives

Construction

Casein glue (Elmers-Weldwood)
Source: Hardware, paint store

Mounting Prints

Synthetic Latex (Atex No. 16)
Casein base (Pictex No. 17)
Source: Adhesive Products, Inc.
1660 Boone Ave., Bronx, N. Y.

Tools

Construction

Miter box (Stanley No. 150)
Source: Hardware or Stanley Tools
New Britain, Conn.

Corner Clamp (Stanley No. 404)
Source: Hardware or Stanley Tools
New Britain, Conn.

Other hand tools
Source: Hardware

Finishing

Rake (Paint scraper)
Source: Hardware

Gilder's tip
Source: Paint store, sign painter's supply

Mat and X-acto Knife
Source: Art store, hardware, paint store

Straightedge
Source: Art store, paint store

Compass
Source: Art store, hardware

Glass cutter
Source: Hardware

Roller
Source: Art store, printer's supply

Paints

"Vinyl" base or "Latex" base
Source: Paint store
(Lucite, Pronto, Super Kemtone, etc.)

Leafs—Powders

Gold and metal leaf
Source: Paint store, art store, sign painter's
supply

Powdered gold (Venus Bronzing Powder)
Source: Paint store, art store

Mat Board

Source: Art store

Wax (Butchers)

Source: Hardware or paint store

Linen

Source: Art store or Utrecht Linens
119 W. 57 St., New York 19

Index